Pathway to Platinum

—developing leaders in Pre-Paid Legal

Brian Mast, with Platinums
Kevin Rhea and Brian Carruthers

insight
PUBLISHING GROUP
Tulsa, Oklahoma

PATHWAY TO PLATINUM

Pathway to Platinum by Brian Mast
with Platinums Kevin Rhea and Brian Carruthers
Published by Insight Publishing Group
8801 S. Yale, Suite 410
Tulsa, OK 74137
918-493-1718

1ˢᵗ printing: 20,000

NOTICE: The views, positions, opinions, methods, claims, representations, or policies set forth are made solely by this book's authors and are not necessarily the views, positions, opinions, methods, claims, representations, or policies of Pre-Paid Legal Services, Inc. or its subsidiaries. Neither Pre-Paid Legal Services, Inc. nor its subsidiaries has paid for or sponsored in any way the authorship and/or publication of this book and has no opinions about the information contained herein. Furthermore, neither Pre-Paid Legal Services, Inc. nor its subsidiaries shall be responsible for any error, omissions, representations, warranties, or claims of any nature set forth in this book. *Pathway to Platinum* is written by and for Pre-Paid Legal Services, Inc. independent associates. It is intended to be distributed only to existing associates and referenced as a training document. This book should not be used in any situation as a recruiting or sales tool, nor should any of the income and lifestyle statements or testimonials contained within the book be employed or referenced with prospective associates and/or members. Any associate deemed to be inappropriately utilizing the book or the contents will be subject to disciplinary action, up to and possibly including termination.

ISBN: 1-890900-45-1

Library of Congress catalog card number: 2003102784

Printed in the United States of America

Table of Contents

Dedication & Acknowledgments

We would like to dedicate *Pathway to Platinum* to all the future Platinums in Pre-Paid Legal Services, Inc.

We also would like to thank the following Platinums, top producers, and top trainers who invested their time into making *Pathway to Platinum* a reality:

Platinums:

Kathy Aaron
Antonio Adair
Fran Alexander
Frank & Theresa AuCoin
Mark Brown
Brian Carruthers
Michael S. Clouse
Michael Dorsey, Jr.
Mark Eldridge
Alan Erdlee
Steve Fleming
John Gardner
John Hail
Bill & Annette Hamilton
John Hoffman
Darin Kidd
Larry & Mary King
Joe Lemire
Larry Lemke
Mike Melia

Steve & Kim Melia
Ken & Shirlene Moore
Ronnie Robinson
Ed Parker
Russell & Carole Peden
Lorna Rasmussen
Kerry Reid
Kevin Rhea
Mark Riches
Dave Roller
Dave Savula
Darnell Self
Nick Serba
Patrick Shaw
Larry Smith
Wilburn Smith
Dan Stammen
David Stecki
KC & Lorraine Townes
Rodney & Thao Sommerville

Top Producers:

Bill Carter & Linda Diesel
Denise Patrick
Patti Ross

Dennis Windsor
Tom Wood

Top Trainers:

Jeff Olson   Eric Worre

Foreword by Wilburn Smith

I have walked the pathway to Platinum personally and observed every person who has reached the same level. My observation is that there is nothing magical about it. It's a choice; it's a decision.

People ask what I did that others didn't do. To be honest, the answer is that I didn't quit. In my mind, I probably quit a few times early on, but I never literally quit. I was hungry in more ways than one.

Prior to Pre-Paid Legal, I was in the grocery industry for 20 years. I was the manager for 16 years because the owner promised me that he would sell it to me when he retired. When he did retire, he sold it to someone else. My life-long dream was shattered!

I quit my dead-end job and for a month didn't do a thing. My cousin, Mike Smith, the first person that Harland Stonecipher recruited to sell Pre-Paid Legal back in 1973, tried to recruit me.

After looking at the company and taking a long hard look at my own situation, I went to work for Pre-Paid Legal on January 1, 1980. Back then, we only did group sales and direct sales—you simply had to make a living selling memberships. I worked real hard but only made $25,000 and had to minus my own expenses. I felt like I had failed. As a store manager I was making $30,000.

It took me a year to learn the selling techniques, closing techniques, etc. The second year, my income doubled. It had taken me 20 years to reach $30,000; now it was only two years and I was making $50,000. I didn't think it was too bad.

At the start of my third year, I got a letter from Harland that said, "I know you had a good year last year, but this year I want you to earn $100,000." That just blew my mind. I had never been around someone who wanted you to do well or make money. The man who owned the grocery store I managed didn't even like paying me the $30,000 that he did. Now I was being encouraged to make more!

Later that year, through the efforts of John Hail, the network marketing approach was introduced to Pre-Paid Legal. I did make $100,000 that third year, and haven't made less since! That is the potential in the company you have joined!

Advice to the new Associate:

To the new Associate I would say 4 things:

1) Don't quit! Keep going, keep persevering, and keep moving forward. It will be worth every ounce of energy you spend. I promise!

2) Recruit, recruit, recruit! Always recruit. You never know who your new recruits might know. Years ago I recruited Dave Roller who recruited Dave Savula, who in turn went on to earn a million dollars his third year in the business! I would never have known Dave Savula if it weren't for Dave Roller.

3) Don't wait around for the "big deal" to happen. Though a large group sale, for example, would be a financial boom for you, don't spend all your energy and time on a large deal that might not come to pass. I've seen people become disenchanted after waiting for so long and decide to quit.

4) Be enthusiastic! Of all the skills that Platinums possess, I see this one skill as the most critical ingredient to your success in Pre-Paid Legal. If you are enthusiastic, you can accomplish a lot more than if you want to analyze everything to death before you take your first step. Get enthusiastic about the product and about the potential of making more money. Part of my enthusiasm is based in my incredible belief in the mission of equal justice for all under the law. People in America need this product now more than ever, and every year the need only grows.

Pathway to Platinum is straight from the horse's mouth: namely from the top Platinums, top trainers, and top producers in Pre-Paid Legal. For those of you who aspire to go to Platinum, this book shows the way. *I consider it a must-read for anyone serious about making it to the top in Pre-Paid Legal.*

Platinum Wilburn Smith, National Marketing Director, Pre-Paid Legal Services, Inc.

Preface by Kevin Rhea

It goes without saying that the rewards—commissions, overrides, residual income, bonuses, rings, jackets, recognition, and more—are incredible at the level of Platinum. The amounts vary in regards to which memberships are sold, who made the sale, the levels of those within your team, etc.

What does not vary, however, is what is required of you to reach the level of Platinum. Pre-Paid Legal Services, Inc. requires that you first reach the level of Executive Director, which includes:

> *3 legs with an active Director in each leg and 75 membership sales in one month—you may count personal sales, non-Director leg sales (you must have 3 personal sales), and up to 25 sales per leg containing an active Director or personally sell 75 memberships each month.*

Between Executive Director and Platinum are the following levels, including their requirements:

> **Bronze**—*1 Executive Director leg or 150 personal sales*
> **Silver**—*2 Executive Director legs or 200 personal sales*
> **Gold**—*3 Executive Director legs or 250 personal sales*

To reach the level of Platinum and beyond, the following requirements apply:

> **Platinum** — *4 different Executive Directors legs or 300 personal sales*
> **Platinum 2** — *5 different Executive Directors legs or 350 personal sales*
> **Platinum 3** — *6 different Executive Directors legs or 400 personal sales*
> **Platinum 4** — *7 different Executive Directors legs or 450 personal sales*

Platinum 5 — *8 different Executive Directors legs or 500 personal sales*
Platinum 6 — *9 different Executive Directors legs or 550 personal sales*
Platinum 7 — *10 different Executive Directors legs or 600 personal sales*

Keep these requirements in mind as you journey down the pathway to Platinum.

Platinum Kevin Rhea

Introduction by Brian Carruthers

At the level of Platinum, life changes, as these Platinums will tell you:

Time with family!

Being a Platinum has allowed me to be able to spend more time with my wife, kids, family, and church. I like being able to do what I want to do when I want to do it. A lot of the time I am the only dad on field trips or eating lunch with my kids.

We can go on vacation and come back when we're ready, not when we have to be back for a job. I can sleep until I'm done. It's also allowed me to dictate what I am worth, not someone else. It has allowed my wife to go from a '89 Dodge Spirit to a new Yukon XL with DVD, VCR, PlayStation, and four TV screens to entertain my kids while traveling.

—*Platinum Darrin Kidd*

Freedom!

Platinum is freedom in every sense of the word: financial freedom, time freedom, relationship freedom, and freedom to make decisions that benefit so many others.

It's freedom to be part of a winning team. You can't reach Platinum without the help of a strong team. The relationships that are developed in the process of becoming Platinum are priceless.

It's freedom to build your future, a future filled with abundance of friends, business associates, and finances. You are able to be with your family when you want to, live where you want to, spend time with the people you want to, and

build your business at the same time…how do you put a value on that? I don't know how it could be any better!
—*Platinum Kathy Aaron*

Getting more out of life!

It isn't about what we have to do; it's about what we want to do with our lives. At Platinum the boss isn't deciding anything for your life anymore. For the first time, you can do what you want to do! It's truly powerful and life changing. You are in charge of your own destiny.

Pre-Paid Legal may not be your passion, but it can be the vehicle to help get you there. If you can't get where you want to go under your current circumstances, then you need to change something! With Pre-Paid Legal you can fund your passion.

My passion is personal development—helping other people reach their dreams. Pre-Paid Legal is an awesome company. I feel like I have a leadership development company and Pre-Paid Legal happens to be the product.
—*Platinum John Gardner*

Helping others!

I was married and had children by the age of 15. People used to call me "poor Frannie," but they don't call me that anymore! Today my goal is to get parents home with their children. That is what motivates me. I used to leave my kids with people I hardly knew and I know what it's like to pick them up and put them to bed and feel bad about hardly seeing them.

I intend to help bring home as many single parents as I can, providing them with the opportunity to be with their children while making an incredible income. I also want to help women my age who think their life is over. They are trying to live on Social Security but can't. The last years should be the best years!

I have a lot of vision to help a lot of people.

—*Platinum Fran Alexander*

Sense of accomplishment and MUCH more!

The sense of accomplishment that you have given to the success of others and helped many people change their lives for the better is indescribable! I've never seen an occupation where you can achieve your dream lifestyle of time and money freedom all because you went out and helped people and had fun doing it. (I guess Platinum means having a great time helping people and getting paid serious money for doing it!)

Just imagine waking up when you are done sleeping, working only because you want to, living in your dream home, driving your dream car(s), personally taking your kids and dropping them off at their school of choice, taking long vacations until you are ready to go home, having people ask for your autograph—not because you scored a touchdown but because you impacted their life.

Platinum means you have become a millionaire in your mindset, not just your bank account. You have proven that you are not selfish and that you are a servant of others. You are a visionary and a leader and you deserve to live like a king or queen because of what you bring to so many lives through your work. You are a professional, a friend, a mentor, and a teacher.

I personally feel that if people are not Platinum in Pre-Paid Legal they may never experience the true sense of freedom and self-worth and passion for living that life can offer. What other job or endeavor offers all of this?

—*Platinum Brian Carruthers*

Seeing others become more than they were!

The money is exciting, but the real gratification is seeing people reach their God-given potential. I enjoy that more than anything. When someone who cares about you sits you down and believes in you more than you believe in yourself, doesn't that impact you in a powerful way? That's why we say, "We are in the personal development business with a great comp plan!"

—*Platinum Patrick Shaw*

Impacting your own life!

Being Platinum impacts your life, your lifestyle, what you can do as a family, where you vacation, what you drive, how you live—all of these things are affected. But the real impact is on the people you work with. To me, that is the joy of the business.

—*Platinum Lorna Rasmussen*

Being Platinum obviously means a lot to these Platinums, but how to get there is what this book is about. Before you read the chapters that follow, honestly ask yourself, "Do I have the vision to be Platinum? Do I want just enough to pay the bills or do I want to buy the house outright? Do I want a reliable car or do I want the car(s) of my dreams? Do I want to go on vacation once a year or do I want to go on vacation once a month? Do I want to give $50 toward a good cause or do I want to give $50,000?"

If you dream of bigger things, like Harland Stonecipher, founder and CEO of Pre-Paid Legal Services, Inc., then this book is for you.

Platinum Brian Carruthers

Part I
BECOMING THE LEADER

Chapter 1—*12 keys to reaching Platinum*

Chapter #1 reveals:

12 keys to reaching Platinum:

#1 - Having a consistently
positive attitude

#3 - Learning to handle rejection

#5 - Slowing down to grow fast

#10 - Embracing the process

And more!

Justice For All

12 keys to reaching Platinum
—the proven principles of the top producers

Reaching the prestigious level of Platinum within Pre-Paid Legal is the dream of thousands of people, but only a few will make it.

Why is that?

It certainly is not because the Platinums are something special. They come from a mixed background, including grocers, schoolteachers, butchers, business owners, policemen, lawyers, real-estate agents, comedians, and broke, unemployed individuals. They started when Pre-Paid Legal had much less training, tools, material, and help than you have today, but they all went on to become Platinums...*and if they can do it, so can you!*

But these top-producing Platinums must know something you do not, right? They must have a hidden arsenal of catch phrases that work with 100% accuracy. Or maybe they have secret information on where the best recruiting markets are.

The truth is, there are no secrets to success in Pre-Paid Legal. These Platinums possess only keys—*proven principles*—that they continue to repeat over and over within their teams. For you to reach the level of Platinum and unlock the opportunity that is in front of you, the same proven principles are what you need.

Here are 12 keys to reaching Platinum:

Key #1—Platinums have a consistently positive attitude

Platinums are positive. They see the good in situations because they look for it. Henry Ford once said, "Whether you believe you can or believe you can't, you are probably right." In short, you will always find what you are looking for.

This positive outlook on life causes Platinums to find what they are looking for: the right recruits, the right relationships, the right leads, etc. That is because, through their positive attitude, they have:

- *Excitement*—they see the big picture ahead, for them, their team, and the company, and they charge forward.
- *Focus*—they stay focused and on track, regardless of what others are saying, thinking, or doing.
- *Stick-to-it-ness*—enables them to keep pursuing a lead month after month to see it bring in tens of thousands of dollars when the door finally opens.
- *Resilience*—no matter what people say, including those whose words mean the most, they keep selling memberships and recruiting more people
- *Belief*—they believe in themselves, in their team members, in the company, and in the service so much that any rejection is considered the result of the prospect not fully understanding the service/opportunity, the prospect being too narrow minded to grasp the value of the opportunity, or the timing being not quite right. Whatever the reason, rejection is never personal.

> **Platinum Advice:**
> "90% of winning is being excited...especially when you don't feel like it." —*Ed Parker*

- *Respect*—they take the high road in life, respecting other people and speaking well of others, even when facts might say otherwise.
- *Encouragement*—they are encouragers of their team members, always looking for ways to strengthen, train, and recognize achievements.

By remaining positive, Platinums press on toward their goals, making their positive attitude impossible to beat! "Attitude is the key to reaching Platinum," Platinum Alan Erdlee points out, "if you have a Platinum attitude from the start you'll reach Platinum a lot sooner, so start acting, thinking and behaving like a Platinum today."

Key #2—Platinums know their WHY

"Don't let anyone steal your dreams," says Platinum Steve Fleming, but the truth is you cannot steal the dreams of Platinums. That is because Platinums know their WHY for being in the business. They know what they want and they refuse to let anything get in their way. In fact, "if you don't have a strong WHY, you'll never be Platinum," warns Platinum Kathy Aaron.

That is a pretty bold statement, but having a strong WHY enables you to run over any and every obstacle in your path. "Obstacles are what you see when you take your eyes off the goal," says millionaire and co-author of *Success in Pre-Paid Legal*, Paul J. Meyer. With a strong and motivating WHY, today's Platinums pressed forward to reach their goals. What happens in the end, Paul adds, is that "whatever you vividly imagine, ardently desire, sincerely believe, and enthusiastically act upon…must inevitably come to pass!"

Money is not the long-term goal for Platinums. "If you only want money, that won't hold you for the long term," notes Platinum Bill Hamilton. "No matter how much you get, it is never enough. What you must be seeking is to help others. Money is the byproduct. You must be there to help others—that is primary. Money is part of the formula, but it isn't the whole formula."

Platinum Fran Alexander says, "One of my most motivating goals is to help parents be home with their children. I was a single mom for years and it broke my heart to leave my children with people I hardly knew. It is my aim to help people become successful in Pre-Paid Legal so that they can be with their children. It's their desire and it's mine as well!"

Clearly, Platinums have a variety of motivating WHYs for becoming Platinum, but none of them focus solely on their own wants, needs, and desires. "It's impossible to reach your own goals without helping those on your team reach theirs," adds Fran. Becoming Platinum is a team effort, which also means that the WHY behind the action is also a team effort.

> **Platinum Advice:**
> "You can trade your time for money for the rest of your life at a job if you want to...but you certainly don't have to!" —*Darnell Self*

"If you don't have a strong WHY for being in the business," advises Platinum John Gardner, "then take some time to be alone and dream again. Define your goals. What would you like to accomplish for yourself and for others? Work on it until your WHY is strong."

When your WHY is strong, everyone else had better watch out!

Key #3—Platinums learn to handle rejection

Platinum Brian Carruthers speaks from experience when he says, "To become Platinum, you must be willing to endure hours and hours of rejections and literally thousands of 'no,' 'you are crazy,' and 'I tried it before and it didn't work for me' answers."

The solution is simple, he advises: "You have to grin and plow through it. If you listen to someone tell you that it isn't going to work and you believe them, then they were right. If you believe more in yourself and your team than these people out there who are telling you it isn't going to work, then you will be successful."

Rejection is not pleasant to anyone, as Platinum Nick Serba admits, "I don't like to be told 'no' either, but I'm motivated by the results." A few—or even a few thousand—such negative responses end up doing one thing for Platinums: *it steels their resolve even more to keep going.* Nick points out, "If I'm going to be Platinum, then I alone am responsible to get there."

His approach is as follows:

1-decide what you want

2-lay out your plan of action to get there

3-do whatever it takes

Nowhere in his equation for success does he leave room for "other people's opinions" or "what I'm told cannot be done."

Though Platinums have learned to handle rejection, it certainly does not come naturally. It is something you learn over time. Brian Carruthers explains his reasoning this way: "It's a game of numbers. You will have a lot of people tell you it isn't going to work, but you need to understand that you might have to go through 20 'no' answers to get the one 'yes' answer you've been looking for. That one person could be your next superstar and you could become successful very quickly."

Brian adds honestly, "One of the greatest challenges is keeping yourself even-keeled after all the rejection. You can't get too excited or too depressed—remain steady. Once you are secure and set, you will be successful."

Platinums take this stability one step further by instilling it into their team. "You need to inoculate them to the rejection they are sure to receive," Brian says. "I try to let everyone know when they first start that not everyone is going to like what they are offering. Not everyone will think it's a 'no-brainer' like you did."

The rejection is a very important part of the process, but as Brian concludes, "Those who can endure the most rejection will make the most money."

Key #4—Platinums build relationships with their team

Not long ago Platinum John Hoffman helped a new Associate, Joy Aden, start in Pre-Paid Legal on a part-time basis. With his help, she made $4,600 her first month! She then started working full-time and no longer takes her kids to daycare, commutes in traffic, or leaves the house when she would rather be home. She is happier now than ever before, and she has developed relationships within John's team that will stand the test of time.

John states, "When people experience the trips, the friends, the edification, the recognition, the sense of purpose, etc., they never want to go back to their old life. You form long-term relationships that last forever, and when they like what they do, they would never go anywhere else."

> **Platinum Advice:**
> "Your success depends on what you settle for."
> —Mark Riches

Platinum David Stecki plainly states, "People will come in for the money, but stay for the relationships." It is this type of long-term relationship that produces long-term income and benefit for everyone involved.

After years of working with her team, Platinum Fran Alexander says, "If you build your team members' dreams, you won't have to worry about your own." When the team is reaching their personal dreams, Fran's dreams will automatically come to pass. "I can't say I totally understand it," she admits with a laugh, "but it always works that way."

Key #5—Platinums slow down to grow fast

It might sound like an oxymoron, but slowing down to grow fast makes complete sense. Top trainer in Pre-Paid Legal, Jeff Olson, says, "You need to sit down with your new Associates and learn about them in your Game Plan interview, go to Fast Start training with them, and stay with them until they are able to stand on their own."

> **Platinum Advice:**
> "Take action to your goals."
> —*Rodney & Thao Sommerville*

The end result is well trained Associates who in turn take the same time to train their new Associates. One trained Associate becomes:

...**2** trained Associates who then become

...**4** who then become

...**8**, then

...**16**, then

...**32**, then

...**64**, then

...**128**, then

...**256**,

...and so on.

Jeff sums it up when he says, "If you will do the little things and your group will do the little things and their groups will do the little things, you will have great success." The problem is that people make things too difficult. "It takes genius to keep things 'duplicatable' and fun," Jeff points out. "It's easy to make things difficult and complex."

Part of this slow down to grow fast mentality ties into personal development. Platinum Darrin Kidd calls this purposeful growth the "Slight Edge Philosophy" and says, "By making small continuous improvements every day, the compounded effect over the years makes an incredible impact! For example, reading 10 pages every day of a good book might not seem like much, but over time you will have read hundreds of books, far more than the average person. Who will have the slight edge at that point?"

Whether it is personal development or a good sales/recruiting presentation, slowing down to grow fast is the way to create unstoppable momentum.

Key #6—Platinums stay in Phase #1

There are four phases in Pre-Paid Legal. "**Phase #1** is where you retail memberships and recruit people to retail memberships and are busy giving presentations," says Platinum Brian Carruthers. "This is the only phase you need to be in."

Platinum Kevin Rhea explains it well when he points out, "When people hit higher pay levels they sometimes change their method of operations and lose their momentum. You have to keep your personal production going and increasing so those in your organization will follow the same pattern and work ethic."

Or to put it another way, as Platinum Darnell Self explains, "As a Platinum, always ask yourself, '*If my team did what I'm doing today, how much money would I have made?*'"

Now THAT is a motivating question!

In **Phase #2**, Kevin continues, "People start spending more time trying to get their organization to produce than taking action themselves. As a result, the production of the entire team slows down."

At this level, Managers start managing instead of retailing and recruiting. Some Managers believe that managing others is their new job or that they are "above" retailing and recruiting. Either way, the team starts to dissolve as the number of sales decreases.

In **Phase #3** people become Directors and for whatever the reason they start directing their Managers. The results of Phase #2 are repeated.

Phase #4, at the level of Executive Director, some people begin directing their Directors. Production drops and progress is thwarted, the same as in Phase #2 and Phase #3.

Instead, as Kevin explains, "Lead by example by being too busy doing your own business. Your sales force will do what you do, not what you say." Platinum Ed Parker agrees and adds, "My goal is to never have anyone out-produce me. After all, if you recruit and sell all day long, it will be difficult for people to catch you."

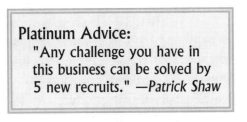

Platinum Advice:
"Any challenge you have in this business can be solved by 5 new recruits." —*Patrick Shaw*

Kevin concludes, "A good example of this is Platinum Brian Carruthers, one of the fastest million-dollar earner in the company's history primarily because he is regularly on the company's Top Recruiter list."

In short, Platinums stay in Phase #1.

Key #7—Platinums live and operate with integrity

Integrity is where it all begins…and ends! Integrity is real and concrete. It is measurable and includes traits like being honest, keeping your word, standing your ground for what is right, and maintaining your honor. It is something you cannot pretend to have. Real integrity is treating others the way you want to be treated—even when nobody is watching.

If your foundation is one of integrity, your choices and decisions will bear that out. On the other hand, if you lack integrity, that too will become evident. As Platinum Patrick Shaw says, "Your actions are speaking so loudly I can't hear what you are saying."

Here are some practical benefits from keeping integrity:

1. increased sales and profits
2. favor
3. a good name and reputation
4. inspiration and motivation
5. respect and appreciation
6. peace and contentment

Writing bad business will only hurt an Associate's overall persistency and long-term income. Platinums understand this and are careful to write good business. Pre-Paid Legal is a company that was built solidly on the foundation of integrity and all Platinums understand that their job is to continue this pattern of integrity.

Platinum John Gardner points out, "There is no need to oversell the membership or to write business that you know will not stay on the books. Always operate ethically, understanding that you are a role model that others look up to. It will always come back to you."

Integrity is a must on your way to Platinum.

Key #8—Platinums always treat it like a business

Platinums enjoy time, freedom, and financial independence. "To have time, freedom, and income requires a good work ethic," explains Platinum John Hoffman, "but

12 Keys to reaching Platinum

it is easy to get into the business and it is easy to get out of the business."

At $249, or whatever special the company might be putting on, the price of entry is so low compared to other businesses that many people do not take it seriously. "If people would treat it like the business that it is, they would do much better," John says, echoing the words of every Platinum.

Platinums take the service that Pre-Paid Legal provides very seriously, they understand the value of the product, and they believe it makes a difference in people's lives. Based on that understanding, Platinums take action.

Top trainer Jeff Olson notes that in franchising you typically invest five times what you want to make. "You will sign a huge contract and pay a lot of money for the franchise and it takes on average five years of hard work to see a profit," Jeff explains. "If you just had a franchise mentality, you would do well in Pre-Paid Legal."

The fact is, Pre-Paid Legal can pay you more than a franchise and it can pay you continual income for life; but the franchise mentality is a good one because it causes you to sell yourself, to build a team, to leverage your effort,

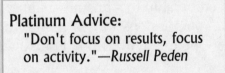

Platinum Advice:
"Don't focus on results, focus on activity."—*Russell Peden*

to study the market and your product, and to work tirelessly toward your goals. Those who treat Pre-Paid Legal like a business have an income that reflects it.

Key #9—Platinums maximize their time

When it comes to time management, every leader in Pre-Paid Legal has two concerns: time spent making

12 Keys to reaching Platinum

sales and time spent developing leaders. Platinums incorporate both into their daily routine.

The making of sales is key in Pre-Paid Legal because sales are what generate the commissions, overrides, and residual income. But before you can maximize your time making sales, "it is crucial that you understand precisely how much your time is worth," notes Paul J. Meyer.

Considering that there are 260 working days in a year (52 weeks X 5 weekdays), if you work 10 hours a day, that is 2,600 hours. Divide your yearly income by 2,600 hours and you know how much you make per hour. For example, someone with a $100,000 a year salary is making $38 per hour.

Paul points out, "You'll notice that whatever number you come up with, it's nowhere near the amount of money you make when you are face-to-face with a qualified prospect who you have time to tell your story to…under favorable conditions…and who has money to buy. That is because time spent in a face-to-face interview pays off five times more than your average entire annual income!"

Platinum Kevin Rhea adds, "I know a Senior Associate who sold two business plans and one personal membership to a businessman and walked out with $542 in commissions in less than 30 minutes! There are very few people with $1000 hourly wages, so spending your time with these types of prospects is the way to go."

> **Platinum Advice:**
> "Plan each day and continually ask yourself: 'What is the best use of my time?'" —*John Gardner*

But in all actuality, most salespeople spend 60-80% of their time working at their desks, filing reports, making sure the paperwork is done and the bills are paid, etc. "They aren't purposefully avoiding their work," Paul explains, "they've just never evaluated the time cost of what they do." Those who do the paperwork are not being paid the highest price, whereas those who make the most money are the ones who have internalized the following 4 priorities:

Priority #1—get face-to-face with qualified prospects (prospects who have already been exposed to the service, have expressed interest, need it desperately, and/or have the right mindset), telling your story, making a presentation, and attempting to close a sale.

Priority #2—be on the telephone, making appointments with qualified prospects and referred leads so you can get face-to-face and make a good presentation with time to tell your story under favorable conditions.

Priority #3—get information about the leads and prospects you are going to call to get appointments to make presentations because the more prior information you have about anyone you will ever call the much better your chances of getting an appointment and doing anything worthwhile with it.

Priority #4—do everything else, though it does matter (i.e. paying the bills, studying the industry, etc.), as fillers in between face-to-face sales.

"After more than 50 years of building marketing organizations around the world," Paul concludes, "all the salespeople I've met or known are only making about half or a third the sales presentations they easily could and are capable of…and should be making. *Their income is therefore half or a third what it could and should be!*"

The objective is to spend as much time as possible on Priority #1 and to spend as little time as possible on

12 Keys to reaching Platinum

Priority #4. That is how you maximize your time when it comes to making sales.

Spending time developing leaders is a constant top priority. Platinum Brian Carruthers states, "This includes teaching your team how to constantly make sales and recruit, teaching those new leaders how to teach their new leaders, giving recognition to those on your team, spending more time with your leaders, being a mentor, encourager, motivator, and more."

Maximizing your time on your way to Platinum means spending your time on two things: making sales and developing leaders.

Key #10—Platinums embrace the process

Platinum Larry Lemke outlines the steps of success that took him to the level of Platinum:

1. Decide what you want and set an absolute commitment that you are going to get it.
2. Become teachable. (Entrepreneurs are creative by nature, so put your creativity on the shelf temporarily. Follow the basics. When you are at a healthy six-figure income, we'll listen to your ideas.)
3. Model successful people.
4. Stay with the basics. (Keep the momentum going—do not back off.)
5. Take inventory regularly. (See if your activities are resulting in what you want—be razor-sharp focused with the results you are getting.)

But instead of just living every day with the goal of reaching Platinum flashing in front of his eyes, Larry, and every other Platinum, learned to embrace the process that is necessary to reach Platinum.

The process is predominately internal, meaning it is the personal development that best prepares you for success. For example, personal development is what enables people to handle rejection, maintain a positive attitude, stay disciplined, lead by example, think long-term, take risks, believe in others, take responsibility for your actions, and manage money wisely. Platinum Ed Parker states, "You can do 99% of the things right in this business, but without a positive winning attitude, you'll fail." Whatever the exact number, Platinums spend time working on themselves for a very good reason.

Shakespeare wrote, "What's past is merely a prelude." It is all a process. Platinum Steve Fleming says, "We have to recreate every day with new dreams and goals of achieving more than yesterday or last year, otherwise we stagnate." The process is all about change, and Platinums know and willingly accept the fact that change is inevitable...and good!

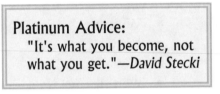

Platinum Advice:
"It's what you become, not what you get."—*David Stecki*

Top producer Tom Wood says, "Our goal is to be financially successful, but we need to enjoy it along the way."

Key #11—Platinums take control by taking responsibility

You can only become Platinum if you are a person who takes control by taking responsibility. Not only do you want that as your temperament, but you want every leader on your team to have the same mindset.

Here are several characteristics of Associates who have such a mindset:

- Focused
- Remaining in Phase #1
- Not complaining
- A team player
- Self-motivated
- Teachable
- A leader
- Accountable
- Positive
- Productive (active is not necessarily productive)
- Self-starter

> **Platinum Advice:**
> "Let me be broke or let me be wealthy, but don't let me settle for mediocrity."
> —Ed Parker

Associates who refuse to take responsibility are, by their own actions, disqualifying themselves from reaching the level of Platinum. Their characteristics include:

- Whining
- Lazy
- Never satisfied
- All talk and no action
- Full of excuses
- Not teachable
- Emotional like a roller coaster
- Always focused on negative
- Self-seeking
- Non-productive

If you have not taken the responsibility and control that you know you need to, then work on those areas. The better you get, the easier it will be to reach the goals you are aiming for.

It multiplies from there because your team follows your lead.

Key #12—Platinums overcome every challenge

That we will face hurdles in life is simply a given. In Pre-Paid Legal, one of the differences between top producers and everyone else is how they handle the challenges in front of them. Top trainer Eric Worre notes from

> **Platinum Advice:**
> "Never accept the failure of others as your own destiny." —*Kevin Rhea*

years of experience, "You can tell the size of a person by the size of the problem that gets them down. When faced with a difficulty, ask yourself, 'Am I not bigger than this?' Then rise up and solve the problem!"

Though there are many, here are 3 common challenges that Platinums have learned to overcome:

Challenge #1—wanting success for other people more than they want it for themselves. "I wanted family, friends, coworkers, etc., to find success," says Platinum Alan Erdlee, "but I finally realized that I wanted it for them more than they wanted it for themselves. It isn't a bad desire, but it is hard to drag someone across the finish line just like it is virtually impossible to push a wet noodle up a hill. If they don't want to change, I can't help them."

The secret, Alan explains, is "to train yourself to work with the willing." Successful people do what unsuccessful people are not willing to do and Platinums know that.

Challenging #2—making things complex. From making a sale to recruiting a new Associate, if it is not simple, then the new prospects will not believe they can do it and sales will not be made. Platinums are masters at keeping things simple because they recognize it is the only way to maintain momentum and multiply their efforts.

Challenge #3—associating with the wrong people. When you venture into business with Pre-Paid Legal, suddenly everyone you know has more than enough reasons why it will never work for you, why you ought to get a real job, etc.

"They are trying to pull you down," says Platinum Ed Parker, "but one of the top reasons why we don't succeed in life is that we listen to our friends, family, and relatives." The answer, Ed says honestly, "is to disassociate from the negative people. Expand your association with likeminded people." You cannot cease being related to your relatives, but you can stop listening to their negative comments. Instead of letting it get you down, do what many Platinums have done and let it propel you to greater success than you—or they—have ever imagined!

These 12 keys are proven principles that serve today's Platinums very well. Allow them to serve you as well.

To those who want to reach Platinum:

When I started, I wanted to make enough money to stay in the business. My short-term goal helped me be focused. I also focused on helping people get in the business who would do the same—take action toward reaching their goals. Getting people productive is what it's all about.

Find out what you want, then make a time commitment, such as two years, and stay focused on it. If you help enough people, you'll reach your goals.

Whatever it is, stay in there and do fundamentals and action will take place. If I talk to enough people about the service, the money will take care of itself. My focus is on the number of people I can talk to. The level and income take care of themselves if you have the right action.

-Platinum Mark Brown

Part I
BECOMING THE LEADER

Chapter 2—*Where it all begins as a leader*

Chapter #2 reveals:

The 5 basic requirements of every leader:

1. selling the service

2. recruiting others

3. plugging into the system

4. promoting events

5. training others to do what you do

Justice For All

Where it all begins as a leader
—the basics of the business

"Work as hard for yourself and your team as you would for a boss paying you a fantastic salary!" says Platinum Michael Dorsey. "In this case, though, the money comes in, continues to grow, and won't go away!"

Financially, through sales, overrides, bonuses, and residual income, you can actually "be paid what you are worth!" Michael exclaims. You will not find many people in life who can say that about themselves, but Platinums understand their financial position.

They also understand that as CEO of their own company, they carry the company's responsibilities, vision, and success on their shoulders.

And you carry the same weight.

Everything begins with the 5 basics

What exactly is required of leaders in Pre-Paid Legal? According to Platinum John Hoffman, there are 5 basic ingredients that every leader must master. These include:

1. selling the service
2. recruiting others
3. plugging into the system
4. promoting events
5. training others to do what you do

In each of these areas, Platinums are comfortable, competent, and confident. How do they get that way? "It takes time to get there," says Platinum Patrick Shaw, but time is obviously not the only factor. Patrick adds, "You need to take action, for with action you gain experience, and through experience you become comfortable, competent, and confident."

Those with the most experience are taking the most action and are therefore making the most money. Platinum Mark Brown plainly states, "Keep at it, keep trying, don't stop. Whoever does the most presentations wins."

That is why every leader must master these 5 basic ingredients on the way to Platinum.

Basic #1—Selling the service

When Platinum Steve Melia first started as an Associate in Pre-Paid Legal, he studied both the presentation and the presenter. "I knew that the people in the front of the room made the most money," he says, "so I made it my goal to know the service inside and out so I could give a great presentation. I also made it my goal to be a likable, friendly presenter that the audience could identify with. Both are part of a good presentation."

Platinum John Gardner adds, "Spend time with people who are successful at selling what you want to sell, then model their behavior."

An obviously important aspect of the presentation process is believing in the service, and the best way to believe in the service is to use it yourself. Platinum Nick Serba says, "My wife and I used the service 32 times our first year because we had two deaths in the family in different states. We believed in the service!"

Not everyone will use the service that many times in a year, but as Platinum Dave Savula wisely points out,

"It's not *if* someone is going to have a legal problem, but *when*."

How true! For example, one Associate, Bruni Mejia from Puerto Rico, has a son who was pulled over 12 times in one day in California, three times with dogs searching for drugs! He was innocent, but he looked suspi-

> **Platinum Advice:**
> "When presenting the opportunity, try to see things through the eyes of your prospects." —*Steve Melia*

cious being just 16 years old and driving a nice car. When Bruni was presented with a Pre-Paid Legal membership several years later, she immediately saw the value of the service because she knows the realities of racial profiling.

For Platinums, it is the stories from Pre-Paid Legal members that continue to cement their belief in the service. Platinum Ken Moore says, "Recently I went into a restaurant where I had sold the owner a membership. She greeted me with a huge smile and a big hug. 'I've been battling the IRS for five years, charged $500,000 and booked for an additional $300,000!' she exclaimed, 'but my Pre-Paid Legal attorney just got it all cleared up. The IRS wrote us a letter saying that we were right all along—the $300,000 bill was canceled and we are in the process of getting our $500,000 back!' She was so excited and talking so loud that the entire restaurant could hear her, but she didn't mind a bit!"

Or consider Daniel Simmons, a member in Florida whose landlord refused to refund his deposit on the house he was renting. A quick call to the law firm and a letter to the landlord and Daniel had his $1000 deposit back.

Stories like these of people getting justice are literally endless, which is why it goes without saying that every Platinum believes wholeheartedly in the power of the membership. It is that belief in the service that makes the presentation so powerful and convincing, even if it happens to be the 500th identical presentation. Platinums do not allow a presentation to get old because they have internalized the truth in a note posted on the door of a theater that read: "Though this is your 3000th performance, this is the first time this audience has seen it." To lose conviction or to lose the newness of a membership is to lose the sale. That is why a high belief in the service is so important.

Platinum Advice:
"You make the opportunity more appealing if your prospects are sold on the membership." —Dave Roller

Platinums are great presenters with a quality presentation. Like Platinum Steve Melia, make that your goal as well—*recruiting will naturally follow*.

That is what happened to Platinum Larry Smith. His first presentation happened to be to a company vice president. When Larry finished his brief presentation, the vice president said, "This is a great service. Can I sell it as well?" Larry admits, "I wasn't even trying to recruit him," but a good presentation combined with the incredible service proved to be an unbeatable combination.

That is precisely what Platinum Dave Roller has found. He says, "I spend most of my time in an opportunity meeting talking about the membership because if people are sold on the membership, there is a good chance that they will buy the membership. And if they are sold on the membership, there is a good chance that they will join the opportunity. You win either way."

Platinum Michael Dorsey leads with the opportunity because, he reasons, "More people want to make more money than want to get a legal plan, but I make

PRE-PAID LEGAL SERVICES®, INC.

AND SUBSIDIARIES

Linda Kedy, Managing Director
Positive Motivational Learning, USCC
Independent Associate/Group Benefits Specialist
Office 770-457-4860 • Cell 770-318-1282
LindaKedy@PrePaidLegal.com • PrePaidLegal.com/go/LindaKedy

Great reading:

The Greatest Networker in the World
John Fogg

Greatest Oppty in the History
of the World   — John Kalench

Winning the Greatest Game
of All   — Randy Ward

sure they see the value in the product before they become an Associate."

So whether you lead with opportunity or lead with membership, making sure your prospects have a clear understanding of the service is vital. It is all part of the presentation process, which leads right into recruiting.

Basic #2—Recruiting others

When it comes to recruiting, Platinum Larry Smith says, "In selecting a good company to work with, everyone must do their due diligence." That is why he recommends that all leaders be able to explain the following 6 points to their prospects:

1. **Is the company credible and does it have the resources to pay you?** As a public company, Pre-Paid Legal's information is public, so you do not have to take someone else's word on the company's credibility.

2. **Is there a genuine need for the product?** All anyone needs to do is read the newspaper to see how many people were being treated unfairly or ask around and see how many people have yet to get their Will done or who need legal advice but cannot afford it, etc. The need is genuine!

3. **Is the product affordable to the masses?** Selling a $25,000 item might make you a sizable commission, but the market for such an item is very small. Selling a $26/month service is something that nearly everyone can afford, which means the market is wide open!

4. **Competition—who are they and can you beat them?** 99% of the people you talk to have never heard of a legal plan. There is virtually no com-

petition and Pre-Paid Legal is without question the market leader.

5. **Compensation—can you make money working the business?** People with various back grounds are making a lot of money in Pre-Paid Legal, which means if you put forth effort, you will make good money.

6. **Timing—is there room for growth?** Our current market penetration is very small and the position for growth is perfect.

"These were the criteria that I looked for," Larry adds, "and Pre-Paid Legal ranks a perfect '10' in every one of these categories." There are few companies that would get such high marks.

After a presentation, Platinum John Hoffman says, "I always ask, 'What did you like best about what you saw?' then I work around whatever it is that they say."

Other questions like "Do you see an opportunity here for yourself?" and "Is there any reason we can't get started right now?" also help focus the prospects' attention on the incredible opportunity in front of them.

One comment John often makes to the prospects is this: "If I could show you a way to double your income, and not jeopardize what you're doing, would you be interested?" Why would anyone say "no thank you" to that question, which is precisely the point! When prospects see the potential and know that

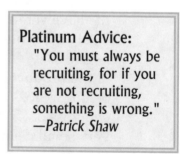

Platinum Advice:
"You must always be recruiting, for if you are not recruiting, something is wrong."
—*Patrick Shaw*

they will be helped to where they want to go, the only logical decision is to become an Associate.

Platinum Dave Savula says, "I give prospects the forms right up front because I assume they want to get

Where it all begins as a leader

40

the membership." And as far as the opportunity goes, top producer Denise Patrick says, "The truth is, they are more afraid than you are! Tell them it's ok. You are with them and will help them all the way along. It's your job to be the leader and tell them what to do. Help them get ready so they can start."

If you make a presentation and do not have time to present the opportunity, take this proven approach by Platinum Larry Smith to prime your prospects for becoming Associates at a later date:

(*To your prospect*) There are a couple things I'd like you to consider. Number one, we work off referrals. I'm sure right now you could work off your mental list and think of some friends who have been treated unfairly like you were, correct? You probably have friends who say they need to get a Will in place to protect their family.

What I'd like to ask you for is a list of referrals. I'm going to contact those referrals the same way I contacted you. Each one of those referrals who buys a membership from me, I'm going to send you a check for $26 for one month's free membership.

Or, number two, if you'd like to see how you could make up to $200 by simply showing this information to other people just like I've shown you, I'd be happy to share our business program with you. Which of these two would you prefer?

This is a real non-intimidating, casual way because the prospects obviously saw value in the service, whether they bought it or not. Larry then contacts and follows up with the referred leads. When someone buys a membership, he calls the person who gave him the referral and says, "I'd like to stop by and bring you a check—when would be a good time to do that?"

Right now is always a good time!

When Larry arrives with his $26 check, he brings the Associate agreement and the membership application as well. He explains, "I know you are not interested in our business opportunity, but one of your referrals did become an Associate and we can set it up in a way that you can benefit financially by his production and his business. I need to put someone's name on this Associate agreement and either you can get paid on what he's doing or I can get paid. Are you sure you don't want to take a look at the business opportunity?"

> **Platinum Advice:**
> "With your prospects, avoid using these negative trigger words:
> - deal/get into
> - sponsor
> - upline/sideline/downline/leg
> - Platinum/Gold/Silver/Bronze
> - business opportunity
>
> Instead, use these general words:
> - "I just started working with..."
> - Director
> - team trainer
> - team
> - corporate overview
>
> Your prospects will think better of you." —*Frank AuCoin*

By asking questions, he is leaving the decision up to them. "Trying to convince people that they need an attorney will never work," he explains. "You have to let the prospects interact in the conversation by creating their own need by you asking them questions so that they can see the benefit of owning this product."

It is all part of the recruiting process and works just as well after a group presentation as it does one-on-one.

Basic #3—Plugging into the system

Plugging into the system simply means that you are utilizing the tools, services, training, and help that Pre-Paid Legal already has in place for you and your team. From conference calls to specialized brochures, from face-to-face presentations to recorded messages, and from videos to weekend trainings, Pre-Paid Legal has gone to great lengths to ensure that the system is in place for your benefit.

In spite of everything, some Associates lean solely on past experiences and past successes to succeed in Pre-Paid Legal. "That is where frustration comes in," says top producer Patti Ross. "In the corporate world, the better I did something on my own the more I was seen as responsible and a good employee. I tried to use those same concepts when I first started in Pre-Paid Legal—and fell flat on my face! I tried to do it all myself and tried to learn everything before I went out and talked to people. It didn't work. That is why people leave the business so quickly. They don't know the answer to questions people ask and they think they should, so they quit."

The secret is to use the system. Patti says candidly, "It took me a while to figure this out, but to my benefit I kept showing up at the training sessions even though I didn't really know why I was there. I heard it over and over before I finally understood...USE THE SYSTEM!"

Platinums utilize the system and teach their teams to do the same. For example, instead of brand-new Associates trying to make a presentation on their own, it is so much easier to invite their

> **Platinum Advice:**
> "People can fail, but a system that is solid and 'duplicatable' will not."
> —KC & Lorraine Townes

prospects to hear someone else present the service and

opportunity. In fact, as Platinum Kelvin Collins explains, "A new Associate has a warm market but should let the upline Manager or Director recruit the warm market because those prospects don't know the upline Manager or Director and will therefore respect him or her much more than their friend."

Unfortunately, those who trust you the most respect you the least. A complete stranger has more respect, so why not let that stranger (your upline Manager or Director) do the recruiting for you? It only makes sense, and as top trainer Jeff Olson points out, "Third-party is *always* more powerful than first-party."

This is all part of using the system that is in place for your benefit. Platinum Kelvin Collins repeats over and over, "My best advice for new Associates is this: don't try to reinvent the wheel. Don't try to add your extra ingredients. Just follow instructions. Clone whoever is successful above you and teach others to clone you."

There really is only one reason for using the already proven system that is in place: increased sales. Since more sales is everyone's goal, it makes sense to take advantage of the system. Using the tools that Pre-Paid Legal has created is one of the best ways to do just that.

Like a Manager or Director speaking to a new Associate's warm market, tools (i.e. video, audio, CD, book, recorded message, etc.) are the exact same. They allow you to put out a professional presentation with no experience. In addition, the tools not only bring credibility, but they also help prospects think, "If that's how difficult it is, then I can do this too!"

Platinums are good at presenting, but they know their business will be limited to their personal growth and time if they do not utilize the tools. "You want to be the messenger, not the message," says top trainer Eric Worre. "The more tools, the more you grow," explains

Platinum Dave Savula, "which is why we always stress two exposures a day and one weekly long-distance package." These exposures and package are simply an audio-cassette, video, or some other tool that explains the service and/or opportunity.

Doing the math, that is at minimum 11 exposures a week. Multiply that by 52 weeks in a year and you get 572 exposures a year, which would result in a lot of sales. Then if a team of 25 people were doing the same thing, that would be 14,300 exposures on that single team! From there it is a mathematical explosion, but that is the power of tools—and the power of the system.

Also, by using third-party tools as "the expert," you can cross any barrier or boundary. Doing everything first-person or by yourself limits you to the people who look up to you and limits your Associates to the people who look up to them, and on down the line. As you can see, and as every Platinum understands, the system in place is good business, so use it to your benefit.

The bottom line is this: the only way to reach Platinum is to use the system. That is, after all, why the system is in place.

Basic #4—Promoting events

Events are seldom in short supply with Pre-Paid Legal. There are Private Business Receptions, luncheons, Super-Saturday trainings, local business briefings, national conventions, leadership conventions, trainings after conventions, and more.

The reason for these events is the same as using the system that Pre-Paid Legal has in place: increased sales! And that is exactly why Platinums promote events or "build" for events. They see the positive results that these events produce and they want that to continue within their team. Platinum Dave Savula condenses the promoting of events down to its purest form when he says, "The bottom line is that meetings make money."

Platinums committed to attending the local business overviews, local events, and national conventions long before they reached the level of Platinum. When they were new Associates themselves, they learned, made sales, and gained recruits through

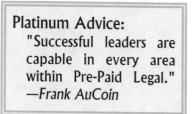

Platinum Advice:
"Successful leaders are capable in every area within Pre-Paid Legal."
—Frank AuCoin

attending and inviting others to the events. To step out of the cycle will do one thing: slow business down.

At trainings and events, for example, statistics show that whoever brings the most Associates will experience the greatest growth within their team. Platinum David Stecki says matter-of-factly, "All we have to do is get a lot of people to the trainings and we are going to make a whole lot of money together. It's not complex— whoever brings the most people will inevitably make the most money. "

As far as events go, the place where Platinums started was with the local weekly business overviews. "This makes everything happen," Platinum Dave Savula says. From there the events spread to Private Business Receptions in people's homes, luncheons, breakfasts, three-way calls, etc. New Associates recognize they want to be independent and do the presentations themselves. They know that the sooner they can grow the business on their own, the better. Platinum Ed Parker adds, "The local business overviews and other local events are how we are able to build nationwide."

Super-Saturdays and other training events continue the momentum, followed by regional and national conventions where Associates get the "big picture" of the power, presence, and purpose of Pre-Paid Legal. An electric atmosphere forms as 10,000 like-minded individuals gather in one auditorium. Again, Platinums know that the Associates who make it to these events have a distinct advantage over those who do not attend...and their results will reflect that.

Platinum Dan Stammen points out, "Attending one event can cut six months off your learning curve. How much is six months time worth to you?" Platinums miss very few events, from weekly business overviews to national conventions, because of the value the events held for them and for their team.

Basic #5—Training others to do what you do

"Duplication is the key to ongoing success in Pre-Paid Legal," says top trainer Jeff Olson. The challenge is keeping everything "duplicatable" because it is so easy to do things that do not duplicate. Keeping things simple is the goal, but it is not always easy. It seems to be human nature to try to make things complex, but the more complex things are, the fewer sales that will be made. That is why Platinums like John Hoffman keep bringing it back to the basics: selling the service, recruiting others, plugging into the system, promoting events, and training others to do what you do.

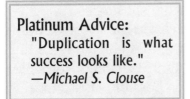

Platinum Advice:
"Duplication is what success looks like."
—Michael S. Clouse

Part of the reasoning behind sticking to the bare basics is that people do what they see, not what they are told. In Pre-Paid Legal, that simply means that your team will do exactly what you as the leader are doing. If what you are doing is producing sales and is able to be duplicated, then you will have duplication and growth. Over and over the process will repeat as your team grows, and that is what this business is all about.

For Platinum Patrick Shaw, the process of training new Associates to do what he is doing always starts with the Game Plan interview. "The focus of the Game Plan is simple," Patrick says, "how to sell a membership, invite/expose people to the opportunity, and get the new person started right. These three areas are absolutely critical for every new Associate."

Patrick explains:

1. *how to market a membership*—every Associate must be able to sit down at any time and do a 15-minute presentation and market a membership with confidence.

2. *invite/expose people to the business opportunity*—exposure is everything. It usually takes four or five exposures before a prospect becomes an Associate. The key is learning the skills that are necessary to walk somebody through four or five exposures. You need to become very proficient at exposures.

3. *getting somebody started right*—90% of training you will ever do with someone is getting that person started right. Get them to Senior Associate as quickly as possible. It is critical to get a check in their pocket ASAP.

Training others to do what you do also includes field training. Platinum Kelvin Collins spends a lot of time with his new Associates making sales with them, as does Platinum Mark Riches. Mark says, "The most effective training is on the job training where the new Associates follow their sponsors around, watching and learning every step of the way." Not everyone will buy a membership, and Mark adds, "New Associates need to see that not everyone buys—and they need to see how you react."

If it is long distance, Mark does a three-way call with the new Associates' top ten influential prospects. Either way, Platinums know that when you spend time with your new Associates, their confidence level will grow exponentially. In the long run, this is precisely what you want, because "the best-trained people will make the most money in the next 5 to 10 years," as Platinum John Gardner states. "Training is key to the military, to doctors, to corporate America, etc. and it's just as critical to Pre-Paid Legal and your team's success."

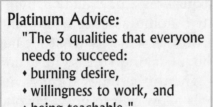

Platinum Advice:
"The 3 qualities that everyone needs to succeed:
• burning desire,
• willingness to work, and
• being teachable."
—Eric Worre

In training others to do what you do, it comes down to this: learn, teach, and then teach others to teach. That is it!

Wrapping up the basics of the business

The best way to sum up the basics of this business is with Pre-Paid Legal's 10 Core Commitments:

1. **Go through the Game Plan interview:** do the Game Plan interview yourself, then do it with your new Associates, and have them do it with their new Associates, and on down the line. The Game Plan interview, described in greater detail in *Success in Pre-Paid Legal*, enables you to connect with your Associates, listen to their goals and dreams, and create a plan of action to reach those goals. Set aside 1-3

Where it all begins as a leader

hours for the Game Plan and do it as quickly as possible with the new Associates while their energy level is high. Nobody wants to be left to "go figure it out" when it comes to the incredible opportunity within Pre-Paid Legal. It is all part of working together as a team, and the Game Plan is the best place to start.

2. **Commit to at least 2 exposures a day**: daily activity, such as handing out two audiocassettes a day and training your team to do the same, is what creates momentum. It is all about taking consistent action with third-party tools. Then it becomes sorting, not convincing, as your tools allow you to grow beyond your backyard.

3. **Attend your local weekly business briefings**: the quicker you can get into a rhythm, the quicker it will become a habit. As new Associates work on their own presentation, utilizing the weekly briefings to grow their business is both painless and powerful.

4. **Send out at least 1 long-distance package per week**: mail it to someone outside of 100 miles from you, and make sure your group does the same. This allows you to build your business across the North America. To find someone outside of your local market, simply pick an area and ask your friends who they know. Say, "I'm wanting to expand in that area" and then send information to whomever they recommend. Stick a note on the tool such as: "We are expanding in your area. I'd appreciate you looking at this. Give me a call." Then follow up on the package you sent.

5. **Attend a Fast Start to Success class**: attend the Fast Start class yourself, then again with your local new Associates. Soak it up. The core people are always up front, taking notes, learning, and returning with their new Associates.

6. **Attend all regional/Super-Saturday events in your area**: Super-Saturdays and regional events. Attend, bring your team, and have your team bring their team. People who do this not only sharpen their skills, but they also have more relationships, growth, bigger teams, etc.
7. **Attend all national corporate events**: you want to be at these events with your team. Your belief grows as you see the big picture and it passes down to those on your team.
8. **Commit to personal development**: read books, listen to audiocassettes, watch videos, associate with positive people, have lunch with successful people you admire, and attend the events. All will work on your personal development. By sharpening yourself, you are arguably getting better and more prepared for greater success.
9. **Find a workout partner**: you need someone who will make you stretch for more—hold you accountable. Look for someone who is strong and who will push you to the next level. As a result, you both will go further than ever before.
10. **Be here a year from now**: commit to being here 12 months from now. That might not sound highly motivating, but settling in your heart that you will be here a year from now will bring a sense of balance to the emotions and criticisms that are sure to come.

"The bottom line is to boil this business down to these simple 10 steps and to get your whole team, eventually thousands of Associates, doing it every day," says Platinum Brian Carruthers.

"Commitment is key!" adds top trainer Eric Worre. "I recommend that you show your commitment by faxing a letter of commitment to the founder and CEO of Pre-Paid Legal, Harland Stonecipher (fax: 580-436-7410)."

You should also post of copy of this commitment letter at home where you will see it every day. However, as top trainer Jeff Olson continually reminds Associates, "What is easy to do is also easy not to do."

> **Platinum Advice:**
> "Become a master at doing a few things every day." —*Jeff Olson*

Like the other Platinums, choose to be a leader who sticks to the basics and who has a well-trained team that also sticks to the basics.

There is always room for another Platinum on stage!

To those who want to reach Platinum:

1. Make a firm time commitment to your business.
2. Treat it like a real career—be your toughest boss.
3. Surround yourself with your upline Executive Directors and learn from them.
4. Attend all local, regional, and national events.
5. Spend 10% of your time in personal development, not PPL development.
6. Set aside an advertising budget, whether it's for leads, ads, etc.
7. Set a strong 5-year commitment to your business!
8. Look for leadership qualities in your team.
9. Take inventory on the leaders who want to go to Executive Director.
10. Work with the leaders who show the strongest desire (by example) to become Executive Directors.
11. Identify a minimum of five leaders in four different front line organizations and 'camp out' with them.
12. Teach them to do the same to become Platinum.

—Platinum Larry Smith

Part I
BECOMING THE LEADER

Chapter 3—*Leading self before leading others*

Chapter #3 reveals:

- Where self-motivation begins

- Answers to your own questions

- Finding what really motivates you

- The 5 principles of a winning attitude

- The bottom line for success

Justice For All

Leading self before leading others
—the unstoppable power of personal motivation

The most powerful force for increasing sales is personal motivation. No single method or idea or promotion can successfully motivate everyone at the same time. Only personal motivation will permanently enable you and your team to become better on the inside (personal growth and development) *and* better on the outside (increased sales, recruiting, leading, training, etc.).

Combine both together and you have unstoppable power.

Where personal motivation begins

"One of the greatest sales errors is to assume salespeople are already motivated to sell," says Paul J. Meyer. If people were motivated to sell, supplying your team with knowledge of the Pre-Paid Legal service, insisting on a certain number of sales, and watching the online sales reports would be sufficient. That is not the case.

The bottom line, of course, is to motivate your team members to greater productivity, but they *cannot be motivated until they are first understood.* You must make an effort to understand them, which is why the initial step of the Game Plan interview is so important. It allows you to discover your new Associate's goals (needs, aims, aspirations, etc.) and then develop plans and strategies to reach those goals. It is all part of showing what is in it for them.

Platinums are genuinely interested in their team's success and overall welfare, not just their own sales, over-rides, and residual income. That is why they take time to know what motivates their new Associates. And the more they get to know those on their team, the deeper the relationships that form. Platinum Fran Alexander says with emotion, "I love my team. They are like family to me." It shows in her actions toward her team and in her team's action.

> **Platinum Advice:**
> "The 3 characteristics necessary for success: a burning desire to succeed, a willingness to get coached and to follow the system, and a commitment to working hard."
> —*Thao Sommerville*

But before you can understand someone on your team, you must first understand yourself. That is where personal motivation begins.

Do you have the self-assurance you need?

Few people possess the inner strength to reassure themselves on a daily basis. Instead they seek for reassurance from family members, friends, employers, etc., **but this is a dangerous place to be.** What if those offering reassurance are jealous? What if they are having a bad day? What if they feel uncomfortable with your personal growth or business success? What if they are not self-assured themselves?

Relying on others for reassurance is unwise at best. Personal motivation provides you with the self-assurance necessary to pursue your own goals without seeking permission or approval from those around you—and this is where you must reside!

Leading self before leading others

The truth is we all need a dependable source of acceptance, approval, and reassurance, but the most dependable source is always yourself. Platinums are self-assured and use that assurance as the basis of their constant encouragement to those on their teams.

Do you know your WHY for being in Pre-Paid Legal?

Are you driven by a strong WHY? Or, as Platinum David Stecki asks, "Does it bring you to tears?" Platinum Michael Dorsey points out, "When it comes right down to it, my reason for being in Pre-Paid Legal is my strongest motivator."

> **Platinum Advice:**
> "You want self-motivated people, like yourself, on your team." —*Paul J. Meyer*

Are your goals clearly defined?

The clearer your goals, the less time you will spend on the obstacles in front of you. Paul J. Meyer states, "Write down your goals in every area of life—financial, physical, social, spiritual, emotional, and mental—in 30-day, 90-day, 6-month, 1-year, and 5-year increments. Be specific. Review your goals every morning and every night. Your attitude will change considerably!"

For example, if you want to be Executive Director or Platinum, write down exactly when you want to reach that goal. Then, practically speaking, map it out, see who is in your organization and where you need to build, and then get to work.

Platinum Mike Melia states it plainly, "Goals give you direction. If you don't know what to do, review or update your goals. Once you have the goals, it is just a matter of 'how do I do this?' along the way."

Leading self before leading others

Do you procrastinate?

Procrastination can exist only where there is lack of something...lack of goal-direction, self-confidence, initiative, concentration, or creativity. The first loss is the loss of action, and from there the team spirals down. Eliminating procrastination will do more for you and your team than anything will.

Platinums do not procrastinate.

Do you see the big picture?

As a person starts in Pre-Paid Legal, typically the amount of time invested is greater than the amount of money gained in return. But over time, the tide turns and the money far exceeds the time invested.

This is an important principle to internalize. You might have questions or have friends and family who question you about how little you have to show for your efforts. Always remember, as Platinum Brian Carruthers says, "You can trade your time for money for the rest of your life at a job if you want to."

Through your efforts, your big picture of success will eventually become a reality—and those who questioned you will be questioning themselves.

Are you posturing yourself to succeed?

Platinum Steve Fleming says, "If we hear a lot of 'no' answers, our tendency is to put pressure on the next prospect." You need to have good posture, which is caring about the next sale or next recruit, but not too much. Or to say it another way, Steve points out, "The person who cares the least is the one in control."

Of course you care about your prospects, but not if they become Associates or buy a membership. You believe in yourself and in the service; what they decide to do is immaterial. Your prospects need you more than you need them. That is posture.

One practical way to build your posture is to have more prospects than you could ever talk to. Become a master at gaining more referrals and more referrals and more referrals—and your posture will become evident.

> **Platinum Advice:**
> "To people who don't have time or money, that is the reason why they need to do this business."
> —*Brian Carruthers*

Another way to strengthen your posture is to steel yourself on the inside through personal development. All in all, being good at what you do creates a posture that prepares you for greater success.

Do you allow any room for excuses?

Platinum Michael Dorsey says, "The people who want it bad enough for themselves will become successful without their sponsor." In short, they leave no room for excuses.

Top Producer Denise Patrick tells of one woman who was recently divorced with two kids under the age of three. One day she stopped saying there was no way she could be successful because of her situation, her lack of money, her lack of a car, etc. She took action and listed all the people who might come over and visit her. The first time, nine people came to her initial Private Business Reception and she sold three memberships.

"Over a year later," Denise says with excitement, "she wrote me a letter saying that she already bought a car and was about to buy a house!"

Platinums Rodney and Thao Sommerville make it plain when they state, "It's not voodoo, it's what *you do*.

Leading self before leading others

You have to put in to get out." Platinum Darnell Self agrees and adds, "If you are at home with nine broke people, you are bound to be the tenth one. If you want to succeed in Pre-Paid Legal, it is so important that you buy the opinions of those who are already successful in Pre-Paid Legal."

> **Platinum Advice:**
> "You have to be callused to the hurts." —*Michael Dorsey*

You will never hear Platinums making excuses.

Are you willing to pay the price?

The learning curve in Pre-Paid Legal is not that steep, but it will still require effort and time. "People hope for the lottery approach where they 'just make it,' but it doesn't happen very often," says top producer Tom Wood. "The great thing is that you would work hard somewhere anyway, so why not spend your time working with a company that will truly make it worth your efforts?"

You hear of Platinums who made $10,000 their first month, but what we are seldom told is what price they paid prior to Pre-Paid Legal that prepared them for such "instant" success.

"What price are you willing to pay for success?" asks Platinum Mike Melia. "It is difficult in the beginning, I'll admit that, but the price you pay for success now is never as big as the price you pay later for not being a success."

Top trainer Jeff Olson often says, "My experience shows it takes bout five years to be a success in our industry, but it takes the rest of your life to fail." Whether it takes five years to be successful in Pre-Paid Legal or not, the point is that more time and effort are always required in the beginning than at the end.

Platinum Steve Fleming notes, "I've watched a lot of people who stuck in there when things weren't going good. They hung on and kept getting better and changing who they were. In the end, they came through the other side. It wasn't a miracle, but rather the choices that

> **Platinum Advice:**
> "I identify leaders as people who are coachable."
> —*Frank AuCoin*

they made along the way to learn the knowledge and skills and information that comes through advance training and hanging in there. If you mix personal development with passion, belief, and desire, you have the makings of something incredible."

Take Platinum brothers Mike and Steve Melia. They made $260,000 their first year because, Steve says, "of all the inner work that had already been done inside of us." They had already paid the price—and it was worth it!

Do you fill your mind with positive affirmations?

The most powerful reminders of your true potential are positive affirmations, which are simply positive declarations of something you believe to be true or something you expect to become true and desire to live by. Affirmations transform your thinking, your attitudes, and finally, your behavior. Their impact on attitudes and behavior help to produce the results you desire.

The most effective affirmations are those you compose yourself. They are based on your goals and describe the person you want to be, the things you want to do, and what you want to possess. When you repeat such affirma-

Leading self before leading others

tions, you build the needed internal confidence and determination to overcome obstacles, accomplish goals, and improve productivity.

Here are a few affirmations:

- I am the #1 recruiter in Pre-Paid Legal!
- I am an excellent presenter and everyone wants to buy a membership from me!
- I am a master recruiter—it is who I am, I can't help myself!
- I make "ten" membership sales a month (include whatever number is your goal)!
- I am a recruiting magnet!
- I am building a huge team every minute of every day!

Write down your own affirmations on 3 x 5 cards to go in your pockets, print them out and hang them on your office wall, tape them on your bathroom mirror, etc. Read them every day and allow them to stimulate you into action.

Are you willing to change?

Most people want to make more money or have more time with their family, but few are willing to go through the process of change required to get what they want. So what is the secret of those who succeed? It may sound simplistic, but successful people do what is not comfortable. They press through their comfort zones and embrace personal development.

Platinum Steve Fleming says, "When you change, everything changes around you." He adds, "I've seen a lot of people brush off personal development, but when they have disappointments about recruits or sales, they quit. If they had worked to make themselves stronger

Leading self before leading others

through personal development, the setbacks wouldn't have fazed them."

"The bigger the ego, the smaller the paycheck," explains Platinum Rodney Sommerville, "that's just the way it is." Being willing to change is not just a statement of humility—*it makes total financial sense!*

Are you committed?

When Platinum Kathy Aaron started with Pre-Paid Legal, she made a 5-year commitment to the business. "The 5-year commitment wouldn't let me think too seriously of quitting," she says. "I've been discouraged and wanted to quit, but I chose not to."

Her commitment enabled her to press through the difficult times and come out on top. It also helped with her team, as she explains, "I told my team, 'I'll be here in five years.' I wanted them to know that I wasn't going anywhere, and it helped." Such a commitment is a great stabilizer for the entire team.

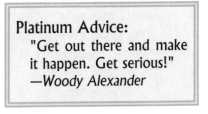

Platinum Mark Eldridge adds, "To achieve the financial freedom and the lifestyle of being able to do whatever you want when you want is worth every ounce of sweat and tears that it takes you to reach it!"

Whatever the goal, only those who are committed will reach it.

The 3 motivations—what really motivates you?

People are motivated by different things, so it is important to pause long enough to ask yourself, "What really motivates me?"

1) *Incentive motivation:* Vacations, recognition, cash bonuses, awards, special parking, etc., are incentives meant to generate more sales. However, incentives have a limited shelf life and over time can actually generate a loss of sales production rather than an increase. There is nothing wrong with offering tangible rewards for outstanding individual effort, but such rewards inevitably become less and less effective when they are expected to carry the primary responsibility of keeping salespeople productive.

What is more, the benefits gained from incentive motivation depend heavily on your want or need at that specific time. This might or might not be to your advantage. For example, if you just returned from a 10-day Caribbean cruise to hear that the new promotion is an all-expense-paid weekend stay in a nearby city, you must admit it would not sound quite as exciting as it once would have.

In the fable of the donkey pulling a cart, the carrot dangling in front of the donkey was a pretty good incentive motivation—but only if the donkey was hungry enough, the carrot big enough, the stick short enough, and the loaded cart light enough. If one of those conditions is not completely satisfied, nothing will happen. Incentive motivation works only when timing and conditions are perfect...and that does not happen often!

The key point is this: ***rewards do not alter your basic approach to making sales.*** Platinums understand this and therefore do not rely solely on incentive motivation to generate sales.

2) Fear motivation: Fear motivation, the exact opposite of incentive motivation, is based on punishment rather than reward. The loss of commissions, loss of status, loss of work, and even loss of personal dignity and self-esteem are thankfully not a part of Pre-Paid Legal. Granted, the fear of losing out on overrides that could be yours if you make it to a certain level do provide some motivation, but like incentive motivation, fear motivation is temporary.

Also, fear motivation does nothing to change your basic attitude toward the service, your prospects, or your recruits. The only way to bring about an internal change lies in attitude motivation.

3) Attitude motivation: The most powerful and lasting force to generate more sales is that of attitude motivation. The reason is that your attitude affects everything, from talking on the phone to dealing with prospects and from how you spend money to spending time with the family.

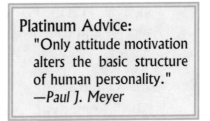

Platinum Advice:
"Only attitude motivation alters the basic structure of human personality."
—*Paul J. Meyer*

Because your attitude is a habit of thought, your attitude is evident in how you react or respond to situations, people, and circumstances. Thankfully, habits can be altered and attitudes can be changed.

"People often have bad habits, which is why Pre-Paid Legal is so appealing," says Platinum Mark Riches, "but unless they identify and break the bad habits by replacing them with good habits, they won't reach the success that is potentially theirs."

It requires effort to be self-motivated enough to change habits. You cannot suddenly have the "right" attitude or the "right" action or the "right" outlook. It takes time. But when you are continually encouraging and motivating your-self—and those on your team—in the right direction, the right attitudes will eventually become habitual.

> **Platinum Advice:**
> "Once you learn the product, 85% of your recruiting and selling is your own enthusiasm."
> —Ken Moore

Of the three ways to motivate others, only attitude motivation creates opportunities, recognizes per-formance, and encourages personal growth. Attitude motivation is the key to unlock maximum individual success and team performance.

Success is a choice!

Attitude motivation is really based on the power of choice. Its essence, as Platinum Larry Smith always says, is this: "Success is a choice!" It is easier to motivate yourself when your habit is to keep moving forward in the face of opposition rather than backing up. Again, it is all about attitude and choosing to succeed.

Platinum John Hoffman says, "Most people don't have an 'I'm going until I make it' attitude and end up giving up on their WHY and going back to their security blanket job." Choosing to succeed is the answer.

"I know people who were so intensely motivated to be home with their kids—tired of getting up when it's dark and coming home when the kids are in bed—that they did whatever it took to succeed," John points out. "Today they work from home and have financial freedom, a goal they chose to fulfill."

5 principles to forming a winning attitude

A winning attitude is arguably one of the most important aspects of sales. When these 5 principles become habitual for you—as they are for every Platinum—you will be unstoppable!

Principle #1—Overcome low self-esteem!

People act as they see themselves. It is impossible for them to act any other way, no matter how much willpower they have. People who see themselves as failures will eventually fail, regardless of their best efforts to succeed,

> **Platinum Advice:**
> "A positive winning attitude is the difference between being good and being great." —*Ed Parker*

while people who see themselves as successes will eventually succeed, regardless of how many times they might fail.

In Pre-Paid Legal, Associates with low self-esteem are convinced their prospects will not buy and subconsciously create the conditions necessary to bring about the result they expect—no sale. On the other hand, Platinum Dave Savula says frankly, "I always assume they are going to get a membership."

Your potential for success is too great to allow an invisible ceiling of low self-esteem to keep you from reaching your goals!

Regardless of need or desire, a low self-esteem restricts the salesperson's perception of what can be accomplished. To escape this negative self-esteem parameter, set high goals for yourself. Add in positive affirmations that have been internalized and you have the makings of a high self-esteem individual who will never be denied again! That positive image of yourself will continue to spread and grow into every other area of life.

"If you find it difficult to maintain this positive outlook," Platinum Brian Carruthers advises, "get help by staying in contact with the people on your team who encourage you and who make you feel strong...and limit your exposure to people who make you feel otherwise."

It comes down to attitude and choosing to form the habits necessary for success.

Principle #2—Never relive past failures!

Remembering and reliving past failures is a common motivational block. No matter how big or how small, past failures are often emotionally charged and hard to shake.

To remove this block, talk about it with someone you trust and walk through a new, positive experience

> **Platinum Advice:**
> "Leave your past sales experience at the door. Be brand new and be a sponge." —*Michael Dorsey*

that replaces the old negative event. In addition, continually feed your mind positive affirmations. Eventually your mind will revert back to the affirmations instead of any past failures.

Inhibitions caused by imagined failures in the past exist only by virtue of secrecy. Discuss these failures as well. When you bring your inhibitions into the light, they lose their impact in your life.

Looking back over past failure is a strange but common quirk of human nature. Inevitably, it interferes with maximum use of potential—our potential that could be applied to future efforts. Since it does no good to remain in the past, close the door on past failures. Learn what you can, but move on by visualizing yourself succeeding in vivid detail and do not look back.

Principle #3—Maintain momentum to avoid complacency

To have a steady income is an obvious goal among Pre-Paid Legal Associates, but a steady income can bring about immobility. Settling down at a certain level of success is common among those who are not continually pushing themselves to excel.

Platinum Brian Carruthers explains it this way:

This business is like an elevator. Some people get off on the Manager floor, some at the Director floor, and some at the Executive Director floor. You can tell when people "get off" the elevator when they stop being coachable and stop doing the little things right that got them there in the first place. It's a shame, because all they need to do is stay on the elevator and keep going up to the penthouse/Platinum floor. I remind people constantly, "If your growth slows down, you were the one who got off at the wrong floor."

Complacency leads to stagnancy, and a stagnant team will not progress. Your team will always follow your lead, so do everything you can to have new purpose, new recruits, and new ideas. That is precisely

Leading self before leading others

why Brian repeats over and over, "Recruiting is the lifeblood of the business."

As Paul J. Meyer says, "You are where you are and what you are because of the dominating thoughts that occupy your mind...no more and no less."

If you are continually increasing your momentum, you will leave no room for complacency, and that is what you want.

Principle #4—Break negative habit patterns

For many people, negative attitudes and habits are a way of life ingrained since early childhood. The result is a tendency to look for reasons why things cannot be done instead of focusing on ways to achieve specific goals.

Attack these negative habit patterns head-on with the same sort of rational explanation offered for complacency and low self-esteem. After all, virtually anyone can slip into the habit of thinking negatively.

Again, feeding your mind positive affirmations will set

> **Platinum Advice:**
> "Investing in ourselves is critical if we are truly going to become strong leaders." —*Larry Smith*

your mind to focusing on what you want to become habitual. In addition, set short-range goals that can be achieved. Every victory will strengthen your self-confidence and build upon your increasing habit of a positive attitude.

Principle #5—Increase your achievement drive

Your achievement drive reflects your desire to get something done. If that desire is lagging, a new purpose and a new goal are needed. Truth be known, there is not a salesperson alive who does not want something! Find something that will challenge you to aim higher, think bigger, and work harder.

Productivity—more sales and more recruits—will increase as a result. As momentum builds, so will your achievement drive. New ideas, new possibilities, and new opportunities will be opened to you.

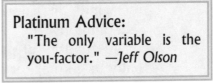

Platinum Advice:
"The only variable is the you-factor." —*Jeff Olson*

Platinum David Stecki says, "It's amazing the doors that open up for you when you have financial freedom and time freedom."

But there is no stopping David as he, like the other Platinums, has a very high achievement drive. Begin working on your achievement drive now. Tool it and refine it so that your momentum continues to increase.

Become a motivator

When it comes right down to it, the only way to reach your goals is to lead yourself. To lead yourself, you must be a motivator. And since you are looking for other leaders like yourself, you are constantly on the lookout for other motivators.

Unfortunately, there are very few motivators out there, as Paul J. Meyer explains:

> I've studied, listened to, and observed sales-people for more than 50 years. Approximately 25% of any given sales team are best described as "unmotivatable." No matter what you do, they continually need your help. It is as if their fire burns out every week and you need to keep fanning the coals.

Most people, let's say 60% of your team, would be considered "motivatable." They burn with excitement, then someone pours cold water on them and their fires dies out. They go from cold to hot, up and down, back and forth, just like a roller coaster. They are affected by the winds of people, situations around them, and opinions.

About 10% of people are motivated internally to go make it happen. They are committed and usually do pretty well, but they are not motivators.

What you need are fellow motivators. Only a small percentage of people, not even 5%, are motivators. These are the leaders who are actively growing their business, growing their teams, and growing individually. They have an "I will not be denied" attitude that stops at nothing!

To become a motivator requires a constant, strong personal motivation. It is fostered through training, personal growth, gaining the right habits, and pursuing a winning attitude...but beneath every characteristic of a motivator is one thing: choosing to succeed.

When you make that choice, you lead yourself. Leading others naturally flows out of that.

To those who want to reach Platinum:

1. Platinum is a by-product of helping others reach their goals.
2. Become a servant-leader—commit to serve and help those leaders who have identified themselves.
3. Go to Ada, Oklahoma to know for yourself what it's all about. It will help you get a passion for the business.
4. Start acting "as if" you were Platinum already (serve others even more!).
5. Become knowledgeable about all aspects of Pre-Paid Legal: CDLP, BOLSP, Group, etc. Even if you aren't interested in them, you can assist others who are interested in that area.
6. Understand that Pre-Paid Legal is only one part of becoming a total person. Earning the money you earn at Platinum is one thing, but to be a true leader at the Platinum level, it is not about how much you make but about how much you keep. You need to be a representative to your team, you need to be a leader, and you need to manage it all.

—*Platinum Bill Hamilton*

Part II
EFFECTIVELY LEADING OTHERS

Chapter 4—*Speed of the leader, speed of the pack*

Chapter #4 reveals:

13 principles to increase your speed:

#2 - Dig, dig, dig!

#4 - Communicate constantly

#6 - Never slow down

#8 - Focus on your 20%

And more!

Justice For All

Speed of the leader, speed of the pack
—because your team will do what you do

When it comes to leadership, sometimes the best place to start is with the bottom line, which is: the speed of the leader will always determine the speed of the pack.

That is logical, but as a leader yourself, what determines your speed?

The answer is simple: *what you know and what you do.* And since the leaders of the sales teams within Pre-Paid Legal are the Platinums, knowing what they know and doing what they do would, of course, make the most sense.

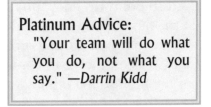

Platinum Advice:
"Your team will do what you do, not what you say." —Darrin Kidd

Here are 13 key principles that Platinums have mastered to increase their speed:

#1—Focus on the Senior Associate position!

Getting new Associates to the level of Senior Associate is the launching pad for success—theirs and yours. Platinum Mark Riches says, "If you can get your people to that level, they will grow and continue. In fact, if every Associate became a Senior Associate, my income would double! That's how much of an impact it makes to the whole team."

With Mark's new Associates, here are the 4 steps that he asks them to take right away:

Step #1—Make a list of 100 names

Step #2—Sort the names and make a list of the top 20 "most likely to buy" prospects

Step #3—Expose those 20 individuals to Pre-Paid Legal. (Mark gives every new Associate 20 audiocassettes or "seeds" and says, "Your job is to get these 20 tapes out in your first 5 days, then harvest for the next 10 days.")

Step #4—Follow up! (Three-way calls, Private Business Receptions/PBRs, meetings, etc.)

"We are teaching this to everyone on our team," he says, then adds, "You need a good approach and you need to build urgency, but don't tell the prospect what's on the tape. If you are standing in line at a restaurant, sitting in your car, talking on the porch, or somewhere else that isn't conducive to conversation, don't say anything. Let the tool do the talking. That's what it's all about."

Platinum Advice:
"Get everyone to Senior Associate ASAP! This gets their money back and proves that Pre-Paid Legal works." —*Dennis Windsor*

"Plan your time with your new Associates over the next couple of weeks," advises Platinum John Gardner, "and make sure they feel free to call you and make sure you stay in touch."

All this helps new Associates to the Senior Associate level, and not only do they have money in the pocket, but they also see that what they have accomplished is all that needs to be replicated. And if they can do it, so can the next recruit! Moving to Manager,

Director, and beyond is within reach—and that realistic view is what you want.

#2—Dig, dig, dig!

Platinum Steve Fleming explains what it means to "dig":

> Let's say you speak with Bob who refers you to John. John says "no" but gives you five referrals, one of which is Jill who also says "no." She refers you to Nathan who doesn't have time but does refer you to Brian who says "yes."
>
> Now you can go back to Nathan and say, "You said 'no,' but Brian said 'yes.' The reason I stopped by is that Brian is planning on going full-time and I wanted to let you know that you could make over-rides and residual income off of his efforts...*if you wanted to.* I know you are too busy, but I thought I'd at least tell you. I have 48 hours to place him."
>
> Nathan signs up. With Jill, she naturally wants to get paid for both Nathan and Brian's efforts, so she signs up. John follows suit, as does Bob.

This "digging" is tiring work, but it is highly effective. Not only do you have five new Associates, but you have five Associates who are "locked in" with Brian's potential success. The more Brian succeeds, the more incentive the others have to become more active Associates and the business grows rapidly from there.

Another reason to dig, as Platinums have learned, is that most of your talent will be deep in your organization. Platinum Mark Riches says, "Some of the top producers in my team have come from more than 12 levels below me. It doesn't matter at all where they are in your team, just find them and work with them. That is why you need to keep digging."

#3—Force no one!

It is impossible to force new Associates to be something they are not. Some will aim for the top and others will settle for a small stable income. The secret is to work with those who want more.

New Associates do not need or want another boss, but they do need help. Since you cannot force them to be or do anything, learn to ask your new recruits, "You said you wanted to be a Director. What can I do to help? My goal is to help you any way I can."

With their desire and your help, they will reach whatever level they want, but they would go nowhere if you try to force them to do anything.

People often say that if you know your WHY, the how will take care of itself. "This is so true," says Platinum Patrick Shaw. "The best thing you can do is to really discover what motivates a person, what their dreams goals and hidden aspirations

> **Platinum Advice:**
>
> "This business is not about 'getting them in,' it is about 'keeping them in.' And they are not 'in' until they are involved. " —*Michael S. Clouse*

are...then show them a realistic game plan that can help them achieve it. Nothing is more powerful than you telling them that you want to help them succeed by using their own reasons to fuel the effort."

Platinum Brian Carruthers notes, "I'm not here to convince anyone. You can't drag your friend or co-worker into the business. I'll try to influence them as much as I can, but I have to work with the willing. This is a number's game."

Forcing someone to do something against their will is never the answer. Paul J. Meyer states, "Just like you can't force anyone to sell, so you can't take credit for anyone on your team succeeding...or for anyone failing. Pre-Paid Legal is a tremendous opportunity that is open to everyone. Those who want it take it—and they deserve credit for their own success."

#4—Communicate constantly!

Whether you are looking for more leaders or calling just to say "hi," it is paramount that you communicate with your team. "I'm on the phone constantly with my team," says Platinum Brian Carruthers, "because I know how important it is to stay in touch. New recruits especially have a way of allowing life's distractions to suck them back into the old routine. Talking to them on the phone helps keep them going."

Brian adds:

> I've spoken with Associates who haven't heard from their Manager or Director in weeks, even months! It's amazing that people who say they are serious about building their business to the level of Platinum don't even take the time to communicate with their team. That one phone call could be what keeps that Associate in the game, and the next person they recruit could be the next Platinum.

> I spend tons of my time just keeping people in the game because at some point they may lead me to a player. The last thing you want is anyone feeling like a forgotten orphan. Only with a team will you become Platinum.

Through communication, leaders help hold their teams accountable. Accountability is a very real factor when Brian tells his team on their regular conference call, "I got my two tapes out today, how about you?" Brian points out, "I don't tell, tell, tell people what to do. I tell them how to do it, show them how to do it, let them try to do it, and then they go do it. And they see me doing it every day!"

It is all part of constant communication—and increased sales—within your team.

#5—Build momentum!

You build momentum with attitude and action. That is why Platinum Ed Parker says, "The leader must always be up, excited, enthusiastic, positive, praising others, etc. You can't ever let people see you down. You must also be leading by example, recruiting and selling all day long." In fact, Ed adds, "My goal is to never have anyone out-produce me."

He breaks the momentum into 30-day cycles, while some Platinums break it into 60 or 90-day cycles. Either way, momentum is being created.

Enjoying the lifestyle that comes with financial freedom also helps to build that momentum. "I make sure people see me playing, going on vacations, coaching by son's baseball team, etc.," Ed points out. "The benefits give them hope and inspiration."

Platinum Kerry Reid says, "I enjoy my home by the ocean and my own schedule now, but when I started with Pre-Paid Legal, I was working 80 hours a week on another job. I created momentum by following Dave Savula's 'two exposures a day and a weekly meeting.'"

Momentum is not based solely on you. It includes your entire team. Moving a lot of tools will help, as will following up with every lead. Platinum Darnell Self says, "To create momentum, you need a Plan of Action. There are 3 steps in our team's push for momentum." They are:

1. **select a squad** (three or four key players)

2. **plan your schedule of events** (weekly trainings, Super-Saturdays, national events, hotels, pre and post events, etc.)
3. **implement massive action** (as a team everyone takes part) "Follow that for 90 days," Darnell adds, "and you'll have more success than you've ever imagined!"

#6—Never slow down!

Recruiting a dud can be a real setback, especially if the recruiting Associate is brand new. It may be difficult to understand why someone would pay money to become an Associate and even get licensed within a licensed state, then turn around and do absolutely nothing.

Platinum Steve Melia says, "This is probably the biggest hurdle for new Associates to get over. They work with someone, help them become an Associate, then watch as everything seems to fall apart."

That is not the end of the story. Steve adds, "If the recruiting Associate would look at the bigger picture, in three to five years, those kinds of people (duds) will not be a concern."

In fact, Steve and his brother Mike freely admit, "We've recruited

Platinum Advice:
"Work an action plan that you would want your leader to be doing; that is when you have become a leader."
—*Dennis Windsor*

70-75 people, but only 20 have done anything, and of that 20, just 10 are the major players within our team." Every Associate needs to adopt the advice: "Some will, some won't, so what!"

Other problems, whatever they might be, can slow you down if you allow them to. Platinum Ronnie

Robinson says, "Don't get stuck in traffic." When people are more interested in talking about things they disagree with or how they were hurt by someone's negative comment than they are in selling and recruiting, then they are "stuck in traffic." The goal, he says, "is to get in the HOV/express lane…and stay there!"

Whatever you do, do not slow down!

#7—Spot leaders quickly!

As much as it would be nice to recruit only leaders on to your team, you have to ask yourself, "What does a leader look like?" Is it a magnetic personality you are looking for? Is it a commanding presence? Is it a loud voice? Is it past experience?

You cannot disqualify prospects because they fail to "look like" a leader and neither can you qualify prospects because they measure up perfectly to your own standards of leadership.

So how do you spot leaders?

Platinum Ed Parker says, "Leaders are the ones who show up, call you, and have enthusiasm. They are the ones who show up at events, meetings, conference calls, etc. They work, spend dinner and time with the family, and are dedicated enough to spend a few hours on the phone at night."

Such leaders make themselves known by their actions. Platinums Frank and Theresa AuCoin point out, "Some of the most talented, well-spoken, educated people don't make any money in Pre-Paid Legal. Why? Because they won't do the basics. Some doctors and business owners won't go to business overviews, be in on a conference call, or send out a CD. They come across as strong leaders, but they don't perform."

The answer is to always be on the lookout for individuals who do what it takes to build their business. That is why Frank can sum up his definition of leadership when he says, "Leadership is earning a commission." Those who make money are the ones who are doing the basics. They are the leaders.

"Actually," Frank points out, "you don't need a leadership-type mentality, but rather a servant mentality of helping others reach their dreams. Leaders are born out of rank and effort, not backgrounds skill level, color, race, gender, etc. If enough people below you succeed, you'll be a leader. It's that simple."

In short, learn to be a "talent scout," and when you find a good one, lock arms and work together.

#8—Focus on your 20%!

In the sales industry, as in everyday life, the 80/20 principle has a way of constantly reoccurring. This simply means that 80% of the work is done by 20% of the people, and when it comes to sales and commissions, 80% of the money is made by 20% of the people.

"On average," says Platinum Brian Carruthers, "20% of your team will do the basics and be workers and 3% will rise up to become leaders." Those are the people that you need to invest your time with. "Spend 80% of your time with these core leaders," encourages Platinum Michael Dorsey. This group of people has the desire and action to grow the business; they are your 20% doing 80% of the business.

> **Platinum Advice:**
> "The internal desire to succeed is easy to spot, but it is difficult to develop." —*Theresa AuCoin*

Speed of the leader, speed of the pack

With the remaining 80% who do 20% of the business, "spend group time with them," says Platinum Frank AuCoin, "or say, 'We'll cover that at the next training or the next conference call or next week's meeting. From a time management perspective, you have to give your attention to the top 20%."

The challenge to your leadership, warns every Platinum, is that the 80% will want 80% of your time, even though they have not earned it. You might be wondering how you can avoid spending time with the nonperformers. Frank AuCoin explains his approach:

> I tell the new Associates: "I know you are exited about the business and I'm excited to work with you. My intensity is going to match yours. If you are serious about the business, you will find that I am a serious support for you. I'll be here when you need me if you are slightly interested, but if you are intense, so am I."

This approach is much like using tools to sort prospects so that you can maximize your time. The difference between the 80% and the 20% is that the 20% take responsibility. "We all have the same opportunity and the same responsibility," says Platinum Nick Serba. "Work with the willing!"

"When I get a phone call from the 80%," explains Platinum Patrick Shaw, "I thank them for calling and ask who we can call right then to do a three-way call with, when we are booking the PBR, or how many new exposures they made that day. When the answers are all zero, I encourage them to take responsibility. They either step up or don't call too often. I have not offended them but put the responsibility on their own shoulders."

In addition, the leaders on your team who make up the 20% are also the ones who benefit the most from your help, training, and relationship. The 80% tend to complain and shift blame, which means your help will be minimally received. Frank concludes, "The people who deserve your time are the ones who are using their time wisely."

Time is one of your greatest investments...invest it carefully!

#9—Help new Associates fly!

Platinum Russell Peden takes what he calls the "Eagle Approach" with his new Associates: "Drop them once, pick them up. Drop them twice, pick them up. Drop them the third time...and if they don't fly, they die."

Russell explains, "With all seriousness, the goal is to get people to be as independent as they can as quickly as they can. For example, I do the initial PBR with my new Associates during their first 10-14 days. Next week we do it again, but this time they do part and I do part. The third PBR they do and I watch. When it's time to do the fourth PBR, I call and tell them, just like I warned them weeks earlier, 'I got a flat tire and won't be able to make it. I know you can do it!'"

From there the Associates fly...or not. Platinum Theresa AuCoin notes, "It takes new Associates three to six months to get comfortable and competent and confident. They can recruit, market memberships, and duplicate, which means in six months the new Associate shouldn't need much help."

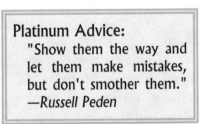

Platinum Advice:
"Show them the way and let them make mistakes, but don't smother them."
—*Russell Peden*

The training is always a process and everyone is different, but the bottom line goal is always the same: *duplication*. Whether it takes two days or six months, new Associates that learn to fly on their own are worth their weight in gold…if not more!

#10—Lose sleep at night!

Platinum Darrin Kidd explains, "We need to be leaders who still lose sleep at night because of the incredible opportunity in front of us! We need to be driven to take action, and if that means we make temporary sacrifices for our long-term gain, then so be it!"

His point is plain: never lose the excitement, passion, and drive for what got you into Pre-Paid Legal in the first place.

Imagine if all the leaders on your team were losing sleep at night because they were dreaming bigger dreams!

#11—Stick to the basics!

Perhaps the most widely used, most successful, stick-to-the-basics presentation in all of Pre-Paid Legal is Platinum Dave Savula's approach:

- *Is it OK if I stop by for 15 minutes?*
- *I have something I want to show you.*
- *By the way, you may or may not be interested.*

Then you show them the membership and sign them up.

Dave's weekly presentations are also very structured: always 55 minutes and always motivational. He talks about the company, the product, the compensation plan, and then how to join. Then when a person becomes an Associate, he says: *"Do two exposures a day and attend a weekly meeting."*

There is nothing complex about that, which is the whole point. Dave notes, "What you do must work. It must duplicate, so keep it simple."

Platinum KC Townes adds, "Model those who already have achieved success and learn to teach others to duplicate those efforts." That is what sticking to the basics is all about.

#12—Help others up!

We all have dreams and things we want to accomplish. The same applies to all the new Associates who join your team. "Find out what *they* want and work with them to reach *their* goals," says Platinum Fran Alexander. "If you want to be Platinum, help your people reach their goals and you'll automatically reach yours. It's a team effort."

The reverse is also true: you cannot reach your goals if you do not help your team reach their goals.

"I believe the goals of those people on your team are more important than your own," Fran adds, but it goes deeper than reaching goals. "If you love

> **Platinum Advice:**
> "Platinum is a position that is earned by helping others reach their goals." —*Alan Erdlee*

them and put them first, you will have anything you want. That's the only way I can explain it."

Everyone wins when you help others up.

#13—Fill your calendar!

Platinum Darnell Self plainly states, "It's impossible to reach Platinum without a full calendar. If it's blank, you have false expectations. Fill every blank with luncheons,

Speed of the leader, speed of the pack

PBRs, three-way calls, presentations, events, weekly overviews, conventions, etc. The only way to get to Platinum is to be in front of a lot of people."

When asked what it takes to have a six-figure income a month, Platinum Dan Stammen explains, "You have to have so much going on, so much activity, that your head is spinning and you don't know up from down, right from left." In short, keep your calendar filled to the brim.

When that is happening, Platinum Brian Carruthers notes, "you are on track to make a million dollars in this business."

The fact is the speed of the leader will always determine the speed of the pack and people will always watch what you do more than they listen to what you say. "That's a given," says Darnell Self, "so you need to always be asking yourself, 'If my team did what I'm doing today, how much money would I have made?'"

Darnell, like other Platinums, takes his role as leader very seriously. From sales to recruits and from personal development to time management, the leader must work on everything simultaneously. "My worst fear," Darnell honestly admits, "is to have my team outgrow my personal development so that I can't inspire them anymore because I haven't grown as fast as they have. I have to keep up and surpass them."

Platinum Advice:
"How many times a day is the PPL story being told on your behalf by a tool or an event?" —Frank AuCoin

Staying in the lead

Robert Kiyosaki, author of best-selling *Rich Dad, Poor Dad*, says, "To be a leader, you must be willing to let go of the old to grasp the new." Whatever change is required of you so that you gain more speed and stay ahead of the pack will be worth it. If it is internal change you face that affects your philosophies, as top trainer Jeff Olson always points out, or external change that affects how you spend your time, as Platinum Frank AuCoin tells his team, *choose to change!* That is the only way to stay in the lead.

Platinum KC Townes encourages all Associates, from brand-new to Platinum, to "gain as much knowledge as you can, consistently set greater goals, and always raise your personal bar higher and higher."

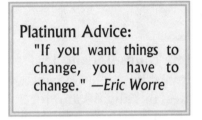

Platinum Advice:
"If you want things to change, you have to change." —*Eric Worre*

To stay in the lead is clearly not a one-time effort. It requires adjustments and focus, but the rewards always make the time well spent. Platinum Bill Hamilton, a prime example of a leader who continues daily to improve himself, condenses his advice for leaders into these 5 steps:

1. Consistently search for potential leaders. Become a talent scout. Foster a keen eye for potential leaders. This is very important because what you want is a team of leaders.

2. Personally, patiently, and persistently work to develop the leadership skills of your new leaders. By invitation, we literally move in with our potential leaders to develop their leadership skills. I've flown to other cities for a week or two, lived with the family, worked the business with them, ate breakfast with them, showed them how to do PBRs, taught them how to lead their team, etc. The effect is tremendous, both in the short-term and the long-term.

3. **Lead by example.** Be where you want them to be: in the Player's Club, on the annual trip because of your high persistency, in the reserved seating, on stage at the events, etc.

4. **Help them to reach higher.** New Associates know what their goals are, but they have room to expand. One of the secrets to developing strong leadership is to help others set and reach even higher goals. They can do it if you help them.

5. **Become more and more counselor and less and less facilitator.** Invest time, energy, and effort in new Associates, but always aim for a "hands free" plow, which simply means that you do not have to hold their hand as much as you did in the beginning. Little by little, back out of the day-to-day role. The timing for this differs per individual, but when your Associates are teaching what you taught them, you do not need to be holding their hand any more, and that is the goal.

It comes down to this: the speed of the leader always determines the speed of the pack.

To those who want to reach Platinum:

Get the slight edge. Get better every day. Plug into the business. Keep the 10 Core Commitments. Be teachable. Work hard—there is no free lunch. Be full-time in your part-time. Know your WHY! It is critical. If your WHY is small, the obstacles will block you out. Be consistent over time. Don't quit. It doesn't matter when you become Platinum—you will become Platinum if you don't quit.

—*Platinum Darrin Kidd*

Part II
EFFECTIVELY LEADING OTHERS

Chapter 5—*Leading your team with vision*

Chapter #5 reveals:

What Platinums envision:

- Vision to sell the vision

- Vision to be wealthy

- Vision to help others to the top

- Vision to recruit nonstop

And more!

Justice For All

Leading your team with vision
—the one ingredient you cannot lead without!

What comes first is always vision. It is the first ingredient in everything we do, whether it is buying a car, building a house, climbing a mountain, or aiming to become Platinum. The reason is that without a vision, you could never reach your intended target!

Vision is what you envision. It is what you "see" in your mind's eye before it becomes a reality—*but if you do not see it, you will never achieve it.*

Helen Keller was once asked how hard it was to live without sight. She replied, "It's far better to be blind than to have sight without vision."

It is your vision that moves you to take action.

What Platinums envision

What is it that Platinums envision? The specifics are different, just as everyone's WHY for being in Pre-Paid Legal is going to be different, but at the core, every Platinum vision will include these ingredients:

- *Vision to have purpose*
"Solid leadership starts with purpose," says Platinum John Hoffman, "because life with purpose is precise and directed, both of which are basic requirements for leadership."

John notes, "I have a plaque on my office wall that reads: 'Ignorance is dangerous because it permits the possibility that we will live all of our lives and never know why we lived.' This serves as a constant reminder to always have a clearly defined purpose."

Practically speaking, where do Platinums get their defined purpose? "It's simple," John states, "it boils down to vision, purpose, understanding your potential, and then releasing that potential."

In short, those who understand their potential are the ones with purpose. They are the ones with vision...and they are also the leaders.

- **Vision to sell the vision**

Platinum John Gardner explains, "In 1976, I bought the first fax machine in Darlington, South Carolina. The circuit court, probate court, and South Carolina Supreme Court in my town used my fax machine for a year before they bought their own. Then in an 18-36 month period, fax machines went from a curiosity to an absolute business necessity. Whatever you call it, the 'S-curve' or the 'tipping point' where an idea takes off, it happened with the fax machine, cell phones, CD players, microwaves, and computers...and it's about to happen with Pre-Paid Legal!"

> **Platinum Advice:**
> "The road to Platinum is about mindset and about having a vision."
> —*Brian Carruthers*

John sells the vision of Pre-Paid Legal. As a result, he says, "I get more recruits than sales because people begin to dream again when they see the potential and vision of Pre-Paid Legal."

One example is Nick Moses, a friend of John's who spent 12 years in the military but found himself push-mowing lawns for a living. Someone showed Nick the

Leading your team with vision

potential of Pre-Paid Legal. His first month he sold 17 policies and traded in his open collar shirt for a business suit.

When he ended up in the hospital for a hip replacement, what would have been terrible for him when he was mowing lawns turned out to be no problem at all. In fact, he sold several policies in the hospital and sold

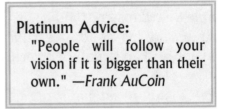

Platinum Advice:
"People will follow your vision if it is bigger than their own." —*Frank AuCoin*

about 20 more policies that month. Within 10 months of joining Pre-Paid Legal, Nick was making $1500 to $2500 a month—more than he had ever made in his life—and with residual income to boot.

Nick caught the vision!

● *Vision for residual income*

Most people "are 90 days away from being broke," says Platinum Frank AuCoin. "The only way to make one dime is to have an asset, and if you are the asset, you are in trouble. Without assets throwing off money to you, you will always be in a money crunch."

That is why Robert Kiyosaki, author of *Rich Dad, Poor Dad*, is constantly encouraging people to branch out into the B (business) quadrant where assets are coming to you whether you are at work or at home or at the beach. He points out, "The richest people build networks, the rest of the world builds net worth."

In Pre-Paid Legal, every Associate is building a network of assets that will pay a residual income indefinitely. "And the better business you write," notes Platinum Mark Brown, "the more you'll make on residuals."

A good example of that are Platinums Larry and Mary King. "We still draw residual income off memberships we sold 20 years ago," Larry says, "Most people would quit using your soap or product after 20 years, but this service is something that people need forever. And if you get sick, the income doesn't go away!"

Platinum Bill Hamilton agrees completely. Being able to will his Pre-Paid Legal book of business to his children and his children's children someday is a strong vision and an equally powerful motivator.

- **Vision to set goals**

Since the goal is to reach the level of Platinum, it only makes sense to take the time to work out a Plan of Action on paper. Platinum Patrick Shaw recommends:

> Give yourself a time frame for what you think is possible, and then work the goal backwards. For example, you might plan to be:
> - Platinum in 5 years,
> - Silver in 3.5 years,
> - Bronze in 2 years,
> - Executive Director in 1.5 years,
> - Director in 90-120 days,
> - Manager in the next 30-40 days, and
> - Senior Associate in the next 2 weeks.
>
> If you don't work out a plan to reach these other levels, you'll never reach Platinum. Once you've set your goal, focus on the most important part and that is today's activity to help you reach the level of Senior Associate. The immediate step is always the most important.

As you are setting goals, you need to ask yourself, "What type of goal-setter am I?" According to Platinum Frank AuCoin, you fall in one of these three categories:

> *A) the pessimist:* These people set the goal for where they already are. They come up with

reasons why they cannot get to where they want to go. They are safe and do not want to be called an idiot for doing something rash or making a mistake.

B) *the realist:* These people set goals that can be reached within a timeframe they set themselves. If the truth were told, 99% of us are realists and fall neatly within this category.

C) *the visionary:* These people set very high unrealistic goals.

"When all is said and done," Frank notes, "pessimists haven't gone any further than the norm, convincing themselves that the distance they came was indeed a goal achieved. The realists hit their goals and are happy. The visionaries, on the other hand, miss their goals completely...but their missed goals are 10 times the nearest competition!"

Vision and knowing where you are going is vital. Frank states, "You can't attract a visionary if you are a realist. You limit who will follow you by your vision, which means if I have the same vision you have, why would I follow you?"

That is a very good question!

Your vision must be larger than everyone else on your team. Platinum Antonio Adair says, "You need to see things long before the rest of the team. Many people don't understand where they are going, but as a leader, you must always have a clear vision so people will follow you."

It is all part of setting goals, which Platinum Larry Smith believes is critical to your success. He says, "You've got to know what you want when you want it and to put a game plan in place that allows you to achieve it!" It only makes sense that every Platinum was first a goal-setter.

- *Vision to be wealthy*

Some people are content to make a few hundred dollars a month with Pre-Paid Legal, but there are others who want to earn six or seven-figure incomes. "The secret to becoming wealthy in this business is pretty simple," says Platinum Larry Smith, but he cautions, "It's not easy, but it is simple."

The secret is to have people on your team earning six-figure incomes. "I look for people who see the vision of what Pre-Paid Legal is and where we are going," Larry points out. "These are the people who understand the timing and treat it like a serious career opportunity."

> **Platinum Advice:**
> "The secret to being wealthy is simple, but not easy." —*Larry Smith*

These serious-minded individuals are also the ones who want to be wealthy and they are the ones willing to change, grow, mature, and learn to reach their goals. "I look for those with the right philosophy," Larry adds. After all, as top trainer Jeff Olson continually states, "If you have your philosophies right, everything else will follow."

When people on your team are earning six-figure incomes, they really cannot afford to go anywhere else, and with the income and lifestyle that Pre-Paid Legal offers, why would they want to go anywhere else? That is where long-term growth, stability, and income benefit everyone involved.

- *Vision to keep going*

Paul J. Meyer had a salesman working for one of his companies many years ago who was "not cut out for selling." However, this individual was persistent, had a positive attitude, and kept saying after each failed sales attempt, "I'm getting better every time."

After 50 presentations without a sale, Paul asked, "Are you sure you want to do this?" After 100 presentations with still no sales, Paul cautioned, "This might not be for you." After 150, Paul told the salesman to seriously consider getting another

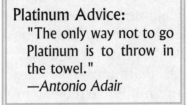

Platinum Advice:
"The only way not to go Platinum is to throw in the towel."
—*Antonio Adair*

job. After 200 presentations without a single sale, the "show was over as far as I was concerned," Paul admits, but the salesman refused to quit.

The 201st presentation was a sale! From that point forward, the number of sales catapulted. "He went on to be the top salesperson in our company," Paul says with amazement, "making over a million dollars a year for five years in a row!"

Most people would have quit long before, but the reward was certainly worth the effort! Platinum Patrick Shaw notes, "I know a couple, Dewey and Judy Gidcumb in Louisiana, who refuse to give up. Dewey once handed out almost 300 Pre-Paid Legal audiotapes with no response, but he refused to be disappointed and continued to look for a better way. Dewey has made many adjustments and went Executive Director in 7 months."

Patrick adds, "Believe it or not, 80% of people who spend the time and money to get their real estate license never sell a single house, and it's the same in Pre-Paid Legal. Success goes not to the swift but to those who endure to the end!"

Platinum Antonio Adair's advice is just the same: "Never give up. As long as you are trying, it's good enough. If it takes six months or six years, you still make it—it doesn't matter."

All of the Platinums had the vision to keep going long before they reached the level of Platinum.

Leading your team with vision

- ## *Vision to be a team*

Pre-Paid Legal is a people-business, which Platinums understand to be the greatest liability and the greatest asset. The "human nature" factor, such as the 80/20 principle, is always a given when dealing with people. Platinums have learned to maximize the asset aspects and minimize the liability aspects.

That is accomplished through "building relationships with those on your team," says Platinum John Hoffman, "which begins first with understanding what each person's dreams, desires, goals, and needs are. You must establish that level of trust."

It is a step by step process, Platinum Kathy Aaron admits, but the benefits are always in your favor. Also, nobody wants another boss, so developing meaningful friendships with those on your team is without question the best possible solution.

Platinums understand what it means to "build the culture within the team," as Platinum Kim Melia explains, through training together, working together, attending events together, providing plenty of recognition, and having fun together. Platinum Frank AuCoin states very seriously, "The culture builds the relationships, for without the relationships, you don't have a team and you don't have future income."

This type of culture and close relationship seldom occurs in corporate America. Consider how uncommon it would be to hear that a CEO of a large company, like Platinum Larry King, is spending his own money to take his top sales leaders on an 8-day, 7-night cruise.

> **Platinum Advice:**
> "Have a clear vision of where you want your team to go and instill that vision in your leadership." —*KC Townes*

From skydiving to special breakout sessions after national events, Platinums have a vision to be a team. They understand, as Platinum David Stecki says, "that people come for the money but stay because of the relationships."

● *Vision to help others to the top*

When your new Associates get started in Pre-Paid Legal, Platinum Fran Alexander states, "you find out their dreams and goals, then help them work toward those goals. Then repeat that process over and over within your team."

> **Platinum Advice:**
> "Look for others who want to be Platinum. Help them be insistent, consistent, and persistent. If they will do that, they will be successful." —*Ken Moore*

Helping others to the top is both necessary and enjoyable. "If you concentrate on other people, you will get to where you want to go," Fran says from experience, "but if you concentrate on yourself, it doesn't work."

She is right in every area, from finances to relationships, because it is impossible to reach the level of Platinum without helping other people reach their goals. Platinum Patrick Shaw is quick to note, "It is your goal to expand the vision of those on your team. It isn't easy, but it's necessary as so few people truly understand what is possible in their lives. Our Creator designed us for greatness but society programs us for failure; our goal has to be to help people to get back to their basic design."

And when people do grasp the vision and begin to rise up as leaders, Fran says, "Give them a chance to grow. When Platinums Russell and Carol Peden first joined our team, Russell was young and wanted desperately to own a Lincoln Towncar. We let him drive our

Leading your team with vision

Towncar because it motivated him to get his own. When he wanted to be up on stage, we gave him more and more opportunity."

Russell does not need any help now, but while he was expanding his vision and growing into the leader that he is today, Fran and her husband Woody did everything they could—recognition, opportunity, training, encouragement, etc.—to help him.

All told, it takes vision to impart vision.

● *Vision to learn*

New Associates are at their lowest level of money earning and at their highest level of anxiety when they first join Pre-Paid Legal. "That is an invitation for failure," says top trainer Jeff Olson, "but as a leader, when you raise their level of knowledge, their anxiety level will go down."

Jeff explains the 4 levels of knowledge that every Associate must go through:

> #1—*learned knowledge*: Study the business, listen to the Power Training, go to the FSTS training, read *Success in Pre-Paid Legal*, watch the videos, and work on having a good, clear presentation.

> #2—*activity knowledge*: The philosopher Emerson used to say, "Do the thing and you'll have the power." That is so true! Work harder and smarter and you will make more money, not the reverse. Continually plan, do, and review.

> #3—*model knowledge*: We are the combined average of the five people we most associate with, whether positive or negative. Minimize your time with some, increase it with others, and delete it with some all together. Associate with the successful people in Pre-Paid Legal and model them.

#4—teaching knowledge: You learn more through teaching than through learning. The winner is the teacher, so if you train your Associates to be teachers, they will learn more as well. The better you can teach your team, the better everyone will do.

Not only are Platinums the best at what they do, but they are always learning and bettering themselves. Improvement is a habit and that is the vision they want to pass on to everyone else. Platinum John Gardner says, "Plan reading time, plan time with people who are accomplishing what you want to accomplish, plan to attend the training events locally and nationally, and lead by example by encouraging others to continue growing and by setting the right example."

> **Platinum Advice:**
> "To maximize your potential in Pre-Paid Legal, you will need to be full-time."
> —Nick Serba

Platinum David Stecki sums it up when he explains, "It's what you become, not what you get."

● *Vision to go full-time*

A lot of new Associates wonder, "When should I go full-time?" The answer is simple: when you can afford to.

Platinum Ken Moore cautions, "Don't go full time until your in most people in corporate America are not happy with what they have; they want more time with their kids and family, they don't like getting downsized, etc. Those who don't want to give up their job are kidding themselves. Who wouldn't want to have more money and more time?"

Usually around the Executive Director level the income is sufficient to go full-time. Many Associates also see how much more they can make by going full-time, but the opportunity is so much bigger than any one person can handle. Platinum Nick Serba states remorsefully, "I've been full-time for years, but I continually feel like I'm not taking complete advantage of the opportunity in front of me."

"The challenge with going full-time is also the beauty of Pre-Paid Legal," says Platinum John Gardner. "Now that you have a team working it's easy to sit back and manage, but when you go full-time you must plan your time carefully, then work as if your entire future depends on it—*because it does!*"

You want as many people on your team with that same vision as possible!

- **Vision to communicate**

    Communication is so very important. It begins with the prospect and continues forever with the Associates. Platinum Dan Stammen begins with success stories, which he believes is "the #1 motivator to get people into the business. When prospects hear of people with similar backgrounds who have succeeded in Pre-Paid Legal, they get excited."

    That is precisely why Dan says, "Everyone must become a master storyteller—*because facts tell but stories sell.* That is why I tell Associates to memorize as many success stories as they can from every tool and briefing they hear."

    Platinum Kevin Rhea points out, "When you are talking to recruiting prospects, tell the stories of your Director or the Platinum above you. Then when you have your own story, tell that. It's even better is when you have stories of those on your team because that tells every new prospect, 'This person is a leader because the team is growing.'"

Leading your team with vision

Communication plays a key part in keeping the excitement and emotional momentum moving forward. Platinum Steve Melia explains, "During the first couple weeks, new Associates realize they have a new lease on life. They start dreaming again and walk with a bounce in their step. How do you keep them excited? By becoming their friend and communicating regularly with them. Your relationship and words are encouragement for them while they are learning how to stand on their own."

As the team continues to grow, Platinum John Hoffman adds: "Gather together as a team to strategize, make Game Plans together, etc. The better you communicate the more those on your team will understand—and take advantage of—the opportunity that they have!"

"Regular and continuous communication is what it's all about," says Platinum Kathy Aaron. "And among leaders, the relationship must be two-way."

● *Vision to recruit nonstop*

Platinums know from experience that new Associates often get discouraged in the recruiting process. They cannot seem to recruit anyone or those they do recruit do nothing. Platinum Brian Carruthers says, "It's like a deck of cards. If you were asked to find the aces by flipping the cards over one at a time, you'd keep flipping even if your first 10 or 20 or 30 cards weren't aces."

That is only natural since a deck of cards has 52 cards and four aces in it. When it comes to recruiting, Brian points out, "People are quick to say, 'Why haven't I found an ace yet? I'm terrible at this. Why did that other Associate find an ace and I didn't? My warm market is no good.'"

Of course all the decks are the same, but some aces are on the top, some on the bottom, and some in the middle. "Eventually you'll find the aces," Brian concludes, "because it's a numbers game." And when you find the four aces in one deck, grab another deck and keep flipping over the cards!

Some people, however, stick with the first deck and try to force a "3" or a "10" into an ace. It is not going to happen! Platinum Larry Smith notes, "Many people continually try to convince or beg their recruits to come to business overviews, attend trainings, go to conventions—all of which would certainly help the new Associates—but I believe that we would be much better off spending that time recruiting new Associates. It's always easier to give birth than it is to raise the dead!"

Brian Carruthers adds, "Grab the new Associate's list, if it isn't being worked, and work it yourself! It's now a warm market to you."

In short, 1) continually recruit, as new recruits are the "lifeblood of your business," according to Platinum Mark Riches, and 2) look for the aces as you recruit. That is the nonstop vision of recruiting.

- *Vision to work yourself out of a job*

Platinum John Hoffman echoes the sentiments of every Platinum when he says, "My goal as a leader is to work myself out of a job by helping create financial independence, time, and freedom in others."

All Platinums understand that the reverse (being needed, unable to leave, dependence, etc.) does not equal freedom. Platinum Russell Peden explains, "If the business rotates around you and it will collapse if you quit, then it's not solid.

> **Platinum Advice:**
> "If your key people haven't changed in six months, you are doing something wrong. We should be developing new leaders." —*Bill Hamilton*

You want to build it solid so that it grows without you. Aim for a walk-away income."

This means that you *do not* want to be the center of attention, always getting all the recognition. "Push the recognition off yourself and onto the leaders on your team," points out Platinum Brian Carruthers, "and you will have created total freedom for yourself."

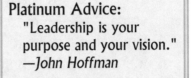

Platinum Advice:
"Leadership is your purpose and your vision."
—John Hoffman

When you help others reach their financial goals, you reach your own.

● *Vision to dream bigger dreams*

Platinum Mary King leaves nothing to guess when she says, "If you haven't reached the level of Platinum or above, it's because your dreams aren't big enough." She adds, "Practically speaking, any dream that you might have in Pre-Paid Legal can be accomplished if you go out and talk to enough people."

Once you catch the vision, it is your job to become the leader to make sure it comes to pass. Such responsibility—*such opportunity!*

To those who want to reach Platinum:

You absolutely must have a strong, clear vision. You also need to be able to handle problems. Don't stress it; go to the solution and fix it. Your paycheck is in direct proportion to your ability to handle problems.

Build the culture in your team through special team get-togethers, events around events, consistent communication, etc. With culture you have relationships and you have a team and you have future income.

—Platinum Frank AuCoin

Leading your team with vision

Part II
EFFECTIVELY LEADING OTHERS

Chapter 6—*What it takes to work as a team*

Chapter #6 reveals:

Why Platinums pay careful attention to:

1. the individuals who join the team

2. what it takes to work as a team

3. how to maximize your team's efforts

4. leaving room for improvement

And more!

Justice For All

What it takes to work as a team
—because your success is limited to your team's efforts

Your team plays a significant part in your overall success in Pre-Paid Legal. Your individual performance is extremely important, but to maximize your opportunity, you need the efforts of your team.

You also *want* the efforts of your team. Not long ago when Platinum Lorna Rasmussen went to Europe with her husband and son for a month-long backpacking trip, she returned with more money in her bank account than she had when she left! That is the power of a team!

As you build your team, pay careful attention to:
1. the individuals who join the team,
2. what it takes to work as a team, and
3. how to maximize your team's efforts.

In Pre-Paid Legal, the leaders who pay the most attention to these three areas are the ones who have the most production, and "production is everything," says Platinum Mark Brown.

1. Individuals who join the team

In addition to the basics of getting a new person started, such as scheduling a Game Plan interview, listening to the Power Training series, attending the Fast Start class, reading *Success in Pre-Paid Legal*, and more, here are several principles that Platinums hold as vitally important:

● *Take responsibility*

To begin with, as Platinum Frank AuCoin states, "It is important to know that your recruits are not coming into business with Pre-Paid Legal—they are coming into business with *you*. They want to know that you are going to be there to help them reach their dreams."

This is a responsibility that Platinums Frank and Theresa AuCoin take very seriously. "When speaking with new recruits," Theresa says, "I tell them our goal:

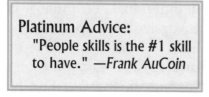

Platinum Advice:
"People skills is the #1 skill to have." —*Frank AuCoin*

'To help you set up your company and put 50 – 500 Associates moving this product for you so that every time one sells, you get paid. You came in business with us and our first concern is setting up a financial firewall around you and your family in case you couldn't work, the money would still be coming into your house.'"

Every new Associate longs for this type of supportive relationship. Though perhaps not stated in those same words, that support is available to all new Associates.

● *Practice checkerboard management*

When you take responsibility for your new recruits, the question is whether or not they will hold up their end of the bargain. "I need to know how serious they are," says Platinum Patrick Shaw, "which is why I give them an initial 'homework' page to complete that includes the basics of writing down their list of prospects, their goals, etc. It's nothing complex, but it is the initial step to see who is serious about the business."

Those who do the basics are the ones you spend time with. "You can only work with the willing," says

What it takes to work as a team

Platinum Nick Serba. The willing Associates "are the ones who show up at business overviews, trainings, conference calls, etc.," Platinum Ed Parker states. "They aren't necessarily the ones with the biggest results, but they are sticking it out, working hard, and dreaming big. They believe they can become financially independent and are willing to work to make it happen—they are the ones I want to help."

The you-make-a-move-and-I-will-make-a-move approach of checkerboard management enables you to work with those who will contribute to the team. "It really is a team effort," Ed continues, "We can't make it alone. Those who aren't willing to go into the market to help their Associates will have a hard time building momentum."

- *Recognize their desire to belong*

  Every person has an innate desire to belong. To use this principle to the benefit of your team, says top producer Tom Wood, learn to:

  1. **Recognize team members all the time**—at meetings, one-on-one, in front of their friends, on conference calls, at big events, when you get an award, etc.

  2. **Create an "Inner Circle" based on achievement**—take your leaders out to a special lunch or dinner once a month. Hold special conference calls and spend time with the people who reach certain levels. Others will see this and want to belong. Unlike traditional business, nobody has to play politics to be a part of the group. They just have to achieve.

  3. **Give people something to do**—not everyone in your team wants to be a top producer. Some people want to run the door or help with audio

and video or develop websites. Some can do both. But give people tasks that they enjoy and let them in on the group for helping you out.

4. **Make people accountable**—call those on your team and ask them what they want to accomplish. Tell them that you will be following up with them to make sure they live up to the promise they

> **Platinum Advice:**
> "Giving recognition to others is a required and necessary skill."
> —*Mike Melia*

made to themselves. Many times we will do more for other people than we will for ourselves.

Platinum Brian Carruthers adds, "Associates want to be part of something bigger than themselves. When they can feel a part of a team that is going to the top, they are twice as excited."

● *Set the right expectations*

Most people who go to college never expect to make a dime during their years of learning, but in Pre-Paid Legal some people expect to be making $30,000 a month within their first 30 days. They have a get-rich-quick mindset that sets them up for a fall.

Though this mindset is not your problem, Platinum Ed Parker notes, "I can't promise people they will be rich, but I can promise them the opportunity to dream again, to be someone their family can be proud of, and to become a better person. But most Associates won't become successful. Most will get tired and quit. Some people will keep going and some day look in the mirror and smile at the person they've become. Those who stick with it will find it to be worth every ounce of effort."

What it takes to work as a team

Platinum John Hoffman agrees when he explains, "People need to hear the potential, but they also need to hear about the price they will have to pay to have the success they dream of. If I sell you on the great muscles you'll get by using a certain exercise machine but don't tell you about the sweat equity you have to put in, I've done you a disservice."

"You can't guarantee anyone anything," Ed concludes, "since it's all up to that individual."

● *Let individuals run at their own speed*

"For full-time people, they should do more than two exposures a day," says Platinum Dave Roller, "but for part-time people, if they just make one presentation a week, they will have results and momentum with that." Those who have more activity will naturally have a higher number of sales and therefore make more money, but pressuring people to have "Olympic-type work ethics can actually turn part-time people off," Dave explains.

Platinum Bill Hamilton says to his new Associates:

> I am as committed to you as you are to you. If you want to be successful in this business and you commit yourself to that and you are willing to do what it takes, then I guarantee you that I will work as hard for you as you will for you. If you want to get to my level, I'll make sure you get to this level.

Bill makes it plain that he will be right there with the new Associate. It allows those who want to run fast to do just that, while at the same time not putting unnecessary pressure on some to perform beyond their level of desire.

The fact is most Associates are part-time, so teach your team that instead of pushing and pulling new Associates along, run with those who are running and walk with those who are walking. When part-time Associates are happy and full-time Associates feel adequately challenged, your team is in a very good position!

2. What it takes to work as a team

Of course, there are many aspects of working as a team that are relevant to your team's growth, but here are several principles that the Platinums see as extremely important:

- *Build relationships with your leaders*

For Platinums, new recruits and new sales are as important as having established relationships with the leaders on their team. Everyone has a slightly differ-

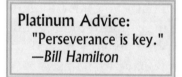

Platinum Advice:
"Perseverance is key."
—Bill Hamilton

ent way of establishing a relationship, but at the core, "You have to work together to get where you want to go," Platinum Ronnie Robinson notes, "so develop a team where you can enjoy success, have fun, and help other people. That is the relationship you want with your team."

From there, Ronnie adds, "Build relationships with your leaders, then help them build the same relationships with their team."

As a result of the relationships you form with your team, top producer Bill Carter points out, "People who want to be around you will do the things they wouldn't normally do. They develop positive like-minded habits. It is called associations and it's part of the relationship."

The team grows and sales increase as a result!

● *Be an encourager*

"Always be an encourager," says Platinum Fran Alexander. "Everyone, whether a new Associate or not, needs tons and tons of encouragement." People crave encouragement but usually get none from their place of employment, so giving out liberal doses of encouragement (not flattery) will go a long way in bonding your team together.

One practical means of encouragement is always being positive when you are on the phone. "If people feel lifted up when you call, they will want to take your call and they will want to have good news for you," notes Platinum John Gardner.

Encouragement includes helping new Associates through the initial phases of growth. "In the beginning you usually give up a lot of time for a little bit of money," says Platinum Patrick Shaw, "but knowing that you will eventually be making a lot more money in

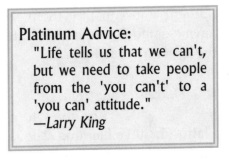

Platinum Advice:
"Life tells us that we can't, but we need to take people from the 'you can't' to a 'you can' attitude."
—*Larry King*

less time is very encouraging! It can be discouraging to hear 'What have you got to show for yourself thus far?' from a spouse or work mate, but knowing that your time will come is the best encouragement that anyone could ask for."

Finally, provide the encouragement for others that you wish you had for yourself.

● *Empower your team*

You empower your team when you develop a level of trust with team members and then "speak to the talents and abilities that are in them," explains Platinum

John Hoffman. "People don't care how much you know until they know how much you care, which to me simply means that it all starts with trust."

Because leaders have the ability to see the talents and abilities in other people, John points out, "A leader who has established a level of trust can build confidence in an Associate's talents and abilities, and that confidence enables the Associate to rise to another level."

Once that trust is in place, your words of "I believe in you...I trust you...I have confidence in you...I expect you to succeed!" are extremely powerful and incredibly empowering. Associates' abilities flourish, motion is enhanced, their desire increases, and they begin taking meaningful action.

"When you empower people, it's the greatest compliment you can pay them," says Paul J. Meyer. "You have created a dynamic climate that in turn contributes to the goals of your team."

● *Share the spotlight*

"Leaders are quick to give away the credit," says Platinum Steve Fleming. The reason is that they recognize the benefit of sharing the spotlight...as well as the danger of hogging the limelight.

Sharing the spotlight encourages leaders to step forward, to take charge, and to take responsibility, just as President Ronald Reagan used to say, "The best way to get something done is to let other people take credit." Platinum Fran Alexander takes a similar approach: "It's all about raising up new leaders. I purposefully try to give people the chance to rise up to meet their potential, and when they do, their business and my business take off!"

Hogging the limelight undermines that completely. "You cannot physically do every PBR, every business overview, every training, etc.," says Platinum Antonio Adair, "and if you do, it hurts you and it hurts your team in the end." By being the center of attention, whether that is doing all the work or not giving others the chance to speak from stage, the team is limited to you, and that is the last thing you want to happen.

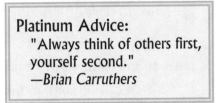

Platinum Advice:
"Always think of others first, yourself second."
—Brian Carruthers

"Your paycheck will be bigger if you give credit to other people," Platinum Mike Melia states plainly. "Freedom comes when your team doesn't need you any more," says Platinum John Hoffman, "because that is a sign of a strong team as well as a sign of a steady income for everyone involved."

- *Be accountable*

Though every Associate in Pre-Paid Legal is an independent Associate, Platinum Patrick Shaw is quick to point out, "No man is an island unto himself. We are in business *for* ourselves, but not *by* ourselves."

Part of what makes the team effort so successful is the factor of accountability. When two people spur each other on to reach beyond their comfort levels, they will inevitably go further than one could have gone alone. That is why having a workout partner (#9 of the 10 Core Commitments) is so important to the Platinums. They understand the power of accountability.

Platinum Brian Carruthers says, "In athletics, the ones who win are usually the ones who get the most discipline. They understand that it is all part of reaching their goals." Whatever the arena, from business to sports, those who are not challenged to get better are not going to win. Brian adds, "If I'm pushing you, it's because I believe in you, and in an accountable relationship, people understand that. Ideally you want a team that holds each other accountable."

It is all part of winning.

3. How to maximize your team's efforts

Much can be said about the many tools within Pre-Paid Legal that are intended to benefit your team. Here are several tips from the Platinums that will help you use those tools and the system more effectively, thus maximizing your team's efforts all the more:

- *Set goals together*

"If you don't know where you are headed, you won't like where you end up," says Platinum Larry King, "so we work with the Directors and Executive Directors on our team to help them set goals and stay on track."

Goals help the team stay focused and working together. "Most people are used to going to work and having someone tell them exactly what to do," Larry points out. "What you have to do is change their mindset to self-motivated and self-driven, and that comes through setting goals together."

- *Make sure the first 30 days are great*

Statistics show that the first 30 days are crucial to your new Associates' success. "The last thing you want them to do is to hit that self-doubt phase real fast," says Platinum Larry Smith. "They'll hit some self-doubt anyway, which

> **Platinum Advice:**
> "Every week select an Associate on your team and help build his or her business." —*Dave Roller*

What it takes to work as a team

is why you really have to spend time with that new Associate during those first 30 days."

The challenge is scheduling time to be with them, go on appointments, make three-way calls, and make sure they are doing the proper activity. "It takes 30 days for people to change their habits," Larry adds, "so if you can get them in the game and break their current habits, they will change." Change is more quickly accepted when money is going into their pockets, so the quicker you can help them make sales the better.

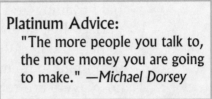

Platinum Advice:
"The more people you talk to, the more money you are going to make." —*Michael Dorsey*

Make the first 30 days a story that can be told to others to inspire them to do the same. You only have those 30 days once, so take advantage of them!

● *Learn how to deal with different people*

In general, there are three different types of people you will encounter in sales: the aggressive person, the insecure person, and the team player. An aggressive person tends to have a big ego and does not like to be told what to do; an insecure person has little confidence and likes to be told what to do; and the team player is confident, accepts advice, and is willing to work as part of a team.

These three individuals need to be handled differently:

> **Aggressive people** need to be challenged. They often say things like, "I've done this before. When can I teach from stage?" Tell them that the best place to begin is seeing how fast they can reach the level of Senior Associate, "if you think you can do it." Ego people have a lot of potential, but their own

ego can be the biggest hindrance to their success.

Insecure people need to know that they will have support. One-on-one support, such as field training and doing PBRs with them, is perfect. Just knowing that you will be there to help them as they learn the ropes is very important to them.

Team players are ready to go. They are confident and can get started right away. Your advice is heeded and they are quick to take personal responsibility. They understand the benefit of being independent while still working as a team.

Platinum Mike Melia points out, "My greatest challenge is dealing with people's egos, whether it's ego-centric (aggressive people) or having a small view of themselves (insecure people). Thinking too highly or too lowly of yourself is the problem, which is why we have a motto that says, 'Check your ego at the door.'"

Clearly the type of people you are looking for are the team players. Over time these individuals will make themselves known, but one quick way to differentiate between the three types of people is in their handshake. Personality tests say the following statistics are common:

Aggressive people tend to turn your hand over with their hand on top when

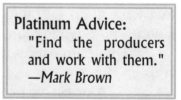

Platinum Advice:
"Find the producers and work with them."
—Mark Brown

they shake your hand. It is psychologically a sign of them stating that they are in control, on top, and powerful.

Insecure people tend to turn their hand under with your hand on top. It is a sign that you are in control and they are not.

What it takes to work as a team

Team players shake hands straight up and down with no turning over or under. It is a statement that they are right beside you as equals.

Those who know how to spot the different people on their team have an obvious advantage.

- **Constantly communicate**

Communicate all the time! Platinum Theresa AuCoin says of her husband, "Frank is on the phone every single day talking with his leaders. The importance of keeping in touch with your team cannot be stressed enough."

Taking the initiative to stay in constant contact through phone calls, voice messages, and emails is a sign of leadership. Platinum Kathy Aaron notes, "It's a two-way street of course, but I make it my responsibility to feel the pulse of those on my team. They in turn do the same with their leaders and the close lines of communication and relationship continue." She understands that you can have no relationship without communication.

Many times, communication simply means being available to provide Associates with what they need the most. "People often experience rejection when they start with Pre-Paid Legal," says Platinum Bill Hamilton, "but not only have we warned them in advance, but we are there to help them through any rejection when it does come."

Platinum Patrick Shaw says, "When I have an Associate who is frustrated with his or her results, we talk about their original goals. And because we originally dealt with their WHY, their goals, and the plan to reach those goals when the Associate got started, it is much easier to deal with the big picture and not get caught up in the little challenges."

Top producer Bill Carter hosts a "structure call" at the beginning of a month for the leaders on his team. To be on this call they must be committed to the 10 Core Commitments and the Players Club. The team members state their goals for the month. Then around the 15th of the month they get back on the phone and see how each person is doing, who needs help, what can be done, etc. They follow that up with another call on the 25th of the month to congratulate those who are on track and encourage the others to keep pressing forward. Active communication like this is powerful!

> **Platinum Advice:**
> "It's all about personal development. The leaders are the ones who have prepared themselves in advance." —*Brian Carruthers*

Clearly there are many more aspects of communication, but the bottom line, as Platinum John Gardner notes, is this: "Your quality of life, more than anything else, is dependent on your communication skills with other people."

Always room for improvement

Every leader could be a better leader. That is a fact, and it forces each of us to humbly work to improve ourselves. In addition, all leaders were once followers, which means they know what type of leader people want to have.

The type of leader you want to become is a leader who is both liked and respected. You cannot lead effectively without those two ingredients. On the way to becoming a better leader, consider these qualities and make the effort to incorporate them into your leadership:

- commitment to getting the job done
- knowledge and understanding of the business of selling
- self-confidence
- controlling your temper
- mutual understanding and respect
- quick, positive decisions

- belief in each team member
- encouragement and support
- credit and praise for everyone who deserves it

If you strive to improve yourself, you will find your efforts reflected in your own performance and in your team's performance. Clearly, your team is affected by you...and your success is limited to your team's efforts. They go hand in hand.

Strive to become the best leader for your team's benefit—and yours!

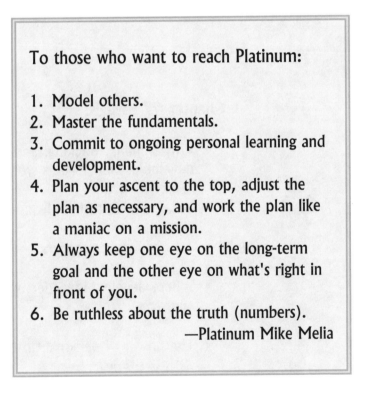

To those who want to reach Platinum:

1. Model others.
2. Master the fundamentals.
3. Commit to ongoing personal learning and development.
4. Plan your ascent to the top, adjust the plan as necessary, and work the plan like a maniac on a mission.
5. Always keep one eye on the long-term goal and the other eye on what's right in front of you.
6. Be ruthless about the truth (numbers).

—Platinum Mike Melia

Part III
DEVELOPING LEADERS TO DEVELOP LEADERS

Chapter 7—*The process of developing leaders*

Chapter #7 reveals:

- Why training, tracking, and developing new leaders works

- What it takes to be a leader

- 10 tips for new leaders

- Where developing leaders will take you

- The power of personal time with leaders

Justice For All

The process of developing leaders
—it is worth getting it right

"The name of the game is developing leaders," states Platinum Brian Carruthers. All Platinums understand the importance of developing leaders. "Without leaders on your team, you have nothing more than a full-time job," notes Platinum Kevin Rhea. "You must have leaders who can run on their own. When that is the case, they are free to make the income and live the life that they've always dreamed of...and you are free to do the same."

You will find, if you have not already noticed, that out of every 100 Associates there will only be a handful of leaders. "We've found it to be about one out of seven," says Platinum Steve Melia, "much less than we had thought or hoped for, but that's just the way it is."

The question to ask is not, "Why are there so few leaders?" but rather, "What am I going to do with the leaders I do have?"

Leadership is a process

Some say that leaders are born, while others argue that leaders are made. Either way you look at it, the Platinums in Pre-Paid Legal went through a process to get where they are today. About that there is no question.

Platinum Patrick Shaw says, "When I joined Pre-Paid Legal, I wrote a letter to Paul J. Meyer saying that I'd be Platinum within the year. He sent me a nice letter that said, 'Don't try to do everything overnight. Leadership is a process.' That meant a lot to me and it helped me understand that it would be a process. It took me two years instead of one…and it was indeed a process."

To make the leadership development process as smooth and quick as possible, Platinums ensure that they provide their new leaders with:

● *Support*

"I find out what their desires and dreams are, and then I help them to reach those goals," states Platinum Ken Moore. "I've learned that if you help them reach those goals and you keep the lines of communication open, they will develop into the type of leaders you need."

But whether Associates run 100 mph or 10 mph toward their goals, they all need your assistance. Obviously you work more with the faster ones as that is better use of your time, but leaders always support their team members. "I will work with everyone on my team to their own degree of commitment," states Platinum Bill Hamilton.

> **Platinum Advice:**
> "When people see you doing what needs to be done, they see how to do it and they see that they need to do the same." —*Patrick Shaw*

Sometimes support means more than help with Pre-Paid Legal business. Not long ago Bill had an Associate who was laid off from her job. "She received $13,000 in severance pay, but was used to bringing home $1,600 a month," he says, "so I called my financial planner and the three of us worked out a long-term plan on how to spend, invest, and save her money."

Support will vary according to your Associates' needs, but being there for them is what support is all about.

● *An example of being the messenger*
"Be the messenger, not the message," says Platinum Brian Carruthers. "It's vitally important that Associates see that they can do what you are doing, such as using a script or showing a video. If prospects think they could never do what you do, then they'll never join the business." That is encouraging and necessary information for every Associate.

With new Associates, Platinum Annette Hamilton (Bill's wife), points out, "We go through our own background and tell them the ups and downs in the business. We tell them that perseverance is key and if they hang in there, it will work out for them."

> **Platinum Advice:**
> "If you show genuine interest in people, they will do things that neither you nor they thought they could do before." —*Bill Hamilton*

Being the messenger is about doing what duplicates, being the message or star of the show is not.

● *First-hand experience*
When new Associates take action, whether they do a good job or not, they are gaining experience, and that is what separates the dreamers from the goal achievers. Top trainer Jeff Olson likes to remind Associates that the founder of IBM was once asked for the secret of success. The answer: "Double your rate of failure."

In short, take action and get experience under your belt. Platinum Dave Roller explains his approach:

At a new Associate's house for the initial PBR, I tell the Associate to introduce me with, "We are glad you are here. Dave is a good friend. This is a great opportunity. This could make you a lot of money."

When the PBR is over and the people have left, I'll have the person sit down with me and give the membership presentation to me. I want just the specifics. When done, if the presentation is bad, I ask for it again. If it's good, then the new Associate is ready to go.

At the second PBR I say, "When you introduce me, explain the membership as well." Before panic sets in, I say, "You'll do fine. Anything you leave out I'll cover." This forces them to do it themselves.

The more experience your Associates can get, the quicker they will be able to make money. Platinum John Hail agrees and cautions, "Help your team, but they need to walk on their own two feet."

● *Respect*

Platinums make it a point to establish a relationship with their leaders that is based on respect. "People first have to know that your intent is good and that you truly care," says Platinum Patrick Shaw. "If you care, you can get away with very strong leadership."

> **Platinum Advice:**
> "Leadership is developing others into leaders."
> —John Hoffman

Patrick, like the other Platinums, has the belief that he would rather somebody respect him and be wealthy than be poor and have that person love him. "There is a balance," he adds,

THE PROCESS OF DEVELOPING LEADERS

The process of developing leaders

"but when people know you truly care about them, they respect you, and that is the foundation for everything else."

Taking your leaders to the next level

It is always time to work with your leaders and help them get to the next level. To that end, Platinums make sure that they are constantly:

● *Spending personal time with their leaders*

Leaders are the ones who "take action, have a strong WHY for being in the business, and make reasons instead of excuses," says Platinum Michael Dorsey. "They are the ones who do what they say they will do."

Michael has found that leaders rise to the top. "When you find them," he says, "invest personal time and build rapport so that you can develop a personal relationship with them." The time you spend with your leaders is always time well-spent.

> **Platinum Advice:**
> "Most people who get excited without adequate training will destroy their warm market."
> —Frank AuCoin

● *Adding fuel to the fire*

Platinum Dave Savula recommends that within your team you:

1. look for the "smoke" (someone who is taking action and making an impact)
2. follow the "heat" (come up beside the active individual)
3. create an "explosion" (add your experience, influence, and passion to the person's efforts)

The process of developing leaders

"Look for people working in your organization, even if they are several levels below you, and go pour yourself into them, " Dave advises, "they will be sure to fire right up!"

Similarly, Platinum Frank AuCoin says, "Go where the sparks are because that is where leadership is developing. You can't spend your time pushing and pulling people who are not doing what they need to be doing. The people who need your time are the ones who are using their time wisely. You can help them most."

It comes back to "working with the willing," Platinum Nick Serba adds, something that every Platinum is good at.

● *Training their leaders*

Pre-Paid Legal has ample opportunities for train-ing. Platinums take it per-sonally and provide the training for their leaders as well as plug them in the system. Platinum Brian Carruthers says, "As much as possible, let the tools do the training.

> **Platinum Advice:**
> "Helping new Associates through the first few steps will build their belief level for the long-term."
> —John Gardner

That allows for maximum and rapid duplication."

Platinum Michael Dorsey agrees and points out that it is important that new recruits understand the three phases of leadership:

> *First Phase*: follow the leaders, learn from them, and do what they do.
>
> *Second Phase*: learn how to teach others how to do the business, a statement that you are becom-ing a leader in Pre-Paid Legal.

Third Phase: teach others how to teach others how to do the business while constantly looking for more leaders.

"Learning, teaching, and teaching people to teach—that is the natural flow of things," Michael explains, then adds, "The third phase is where you want to be because that is where freedom and time come."

● *Always looking for more leaders*

People who take action are the exact type of people you are looking for. They have an internal self-motivation that drives them to succeed. The only problem is that you cannot find them by relying on their outside appearances. You must continually keep an eye out for these aspiring leaders.

When you find them, the development process begins.

● *Tracking the team to develop the leaders*

"We should always be taking 'inventory' of our sales Associates to see who is ready to go to a six-figure income," Platinum Larry Smith notes. "At that point, we team up with those individuals and ensure they truly understand the vision and what it can mean to their family!"

To do just that, Larry spends time with the potential six-figure income earners and shows them the importance of continually taking inventory, looking for the people who are doing the right things, and continuing their leadership development. Larry takes leadership development very seriously and has learned to pour himself into like-minded people. He monitors his

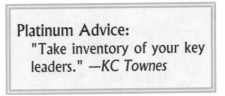

Platinum Advice:
"Take inventory of your key leaders." —*KC Townes*

leaders and knows who is up and who is down so that he

knows exactly where to go, what to do, and who needs help.

After all, as Platinums have found, only those who can measure it can manage it.

● *Developing new leaders*

"You want to develop new leaders," says Platinum Kevin Rhea. "Platinums strive to develop leaders because leaders are the ones who are reaching their goals, and the more people you have on your team who are reaching their goals the better off everyone will be."

Part of developing leaders obviously means looking for new leaders, but it also means developing the leaders you do have. Platinum John Hoffman points out, "You have a tremendous responsibility to help those on your team develop their leadership potential." Top produc-

> **Platinum Advice:**
> "If your goals are clearly defined, rejection becomes a non-issue." —*John Gardner*

ers Bill Carter and Linda Diesel add, "Once you accept the fact that you are a leader, your responsibility is to help others develop into a leadership role."

The teams that are developing more leaders are the teams that will experience the greatest amount of growth over time. Paul J. Meyer sums it up when he says, "Those who develop leaders are the ones who not only understand the power of multiplication, but they are also the ones who will benefit the most from multiplication."

What it takes to be a leader

Just what does it take to be a leader in Pre-Paid Legal? The requirements for leadership are not restricted in any way—they are simply reserved for those who want them bad enough. Steve Melia points out, "Platinums are the ones who want it the most."

The following requirements are what define the leaders in Pre-Paid Legal:

● *Vision*

"Without a vision, people perish," says John Gardner, quoting the Bible. "But I believe that with a vision and the Pre-Paid Legal opportunity, we can soar beyond our wildest dreams!"

John points out that leaders must have a vision that supersedes the common dream-stealers, which include:

1) *The cares of life:* daily concerns often weigh people down, preoccupy their thinking, and effectively minimize any thinking outside the box.

2) *Criticism toward the company:* belief in the company and product are vital, but when a newspaper article, lawsuit, or statement is negative, all belief and faith goes out the window.

3) *Listening to the wrong people:* negative people have an uncanny way of ruining everything, and those who listen to their negativity will fall victim to it.

Those with vision will not let anything or anyone get in their way. The greater your vision, the greater your ability to lead!

● *Action*

"Leaders are the ones making large commissions," says top producer Dennis Windsor, "and though they come from all backgrounds, they persistently worked proven methods to create the commissions that turned them into leaders."

It comes down to action, which includes both making sales and recruiting. Any Associate with a lot of consistent action will be a leader. That is a given!

● *Patience*

"It takes about a year for someone to become a leader in Pre-Paid Legal," note Platinums Frank and Theresa AuCoin. "If they are in the industry and they know what to do to evolve as a leader, it's much quicker, but it is still a process."

Part of that process is learning how to lead a team. Frank explains, "Leaders need to set up their own conference calls, set up their own training, huddle with their team after events, host dinners, lunches, and breakfasts, hold breakout meetings, etc. When this is in place, the team can

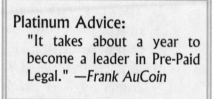

Platinum Advice:
"It takes about a year to become a leader in Pre-Paid Legal." —*Frank AuCoin*

grow into a massive or national organization."

Theresa adds, "Until a person becomes a leader, he or she will never be able to expand the business as much as it could."

● *Planning*

"To get to Platinum, you have to be a leader," notes Platinum Brian Carruthers, "and leaders do what others are not willing to do." Part of doing what others are not willing to do includes taking action that is calculated. Planning is key.

For example, to be Platinum, four Executive Directors are required in four different legs. Brian explains, "You have to find people who are willing, coachable, and who want what you want. If you find four, you have your ingredients for Platinum. Without the ingredients, you can't bake the cake."

Planning must always be supported with action, and that is what makes planning so important.

● *Time management*
You cannot organize time—it is already organized into seconds, minutes, hours, days, weeks, months, and years just fine—but you can organize your use of time. "We are the ones responsible for how we use our time," states Platinum Kevin Rhea. "The truth is, there isn't a Platinum in Pre-Paid Legal with more than 24 hours in a day. We have had and always will have all the time there is...all we can do is use our time more effectively."

Becoming time conscious is therefore extremely important for everyone aspiring to the level of Platinum, and since membership sales are what generate money in Pre-Paid Legal, the best place

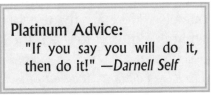

Platinum Advice:
"If you say you will do it, then do it!" —*Darnell Self*

to manage time is with your prospects. Here are 5 keys to maximizing your time with your prospects:

1) *Cut out the small talk*—get into your presentation as quickly as possible.

2) *Boil down your presentation*—time yourself to see just how long it takes, then eliminate any frills.

3) *Keep your sales tools in order*—every minute counts.

4) *Talk to qualified prospects only*—if a prospect does not qualify, move on.

5) *Minimize your travel time*—schedule your driving time when traffic is lightest and make appointments in advance.

The process of developing leaders

● *Attitude*

"I have adopted an I-will-not-be-denied attitude that simply refuses to give up," says Platinum John Gardner. "Regardless of background or experience, you can excel in Pre-Paid Legal if you have an attitude that flat out refuses to quit."

Combine this positive attitude, which will carry you over every obstacle in your path, with the other ingredients of being a leader and you will be unbeatable!

Tips for the new leaders

Hindsight is always 20/20. Fortunately, that is the perspective that Platinums have, to the benefit of everyone else. Here are the top 10 tips from the Platinums on what is required to reach the level of Platinum:

Tip #1—Focus on the daily disciplines

"What you do today you'll see the results 45-60 days from now," states Platinum Michael Dorsey, "so focus on the daily disciplines and it will get done. Your ultimate big picture goal keeps you going, but it's today's actions that will get you to your goals."

Platinums Rodney & Thao Sommerville add, "It's not hocus-pocus, just *focus.*"

Tip #2—Watch your words

"Most of your prospective recruits have a job, so be careful of the words that might scare them off," warns Platinum Ed Parker. "Words like 'deal,' 'leg,' 'downline,' and 'upline' will often keep you away from making a presentation."

The answer is to be normal, be their friend, and see if they are keeping their options open. The fact that you are professional, work with a New York Stock Exchange company, and have ample documentation is a good sign. "Those who use the professional language with no hype have better results," Ed points out. "There is a lot to learn in this business of what to do and what not to do. A lot of it comes down to your delivery—simply your language and how you act with other people."

Tip #3—Spend 80% of your time with your core leaders
"People are either leaders or 'links'—links to the next leader—so you have to work with them long enough to find the next leader," explains Platinum Michael Dorsey. "And when you find those who are doing the right things, you have your core leaders. I talk to them almost everyday and work with them on a personal level."

Spending 80% of your time with your core leaders is wise. "You have to prioritize your time," says Platinum Nick Serba. In a nutshell, that means focusing on what makes sales, gains recruits, and builds the team. It also means not spending time on things that do not bring

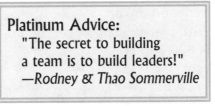

Platinum Advice:
"The secret to building a team is to build leaders!"
—*Rodney & Thao Sommerville*

a return. "You trade your life for your time," Nick points out, "so you need to refocus your time if you aren't getting a good return on your investment."

Tip #4—Serve your team
An important part of leading is serving those on your team. You have a motivating WHY for being in Pre-Paid Legal, but "without a team, you'll never get to the Platinum level," Platinum Brian Carruthers states.

Leading also includes helping others reach their goals, making lasting friendships with your team members, and giving of your own time and energy. "If you have a leader who wants only the money, it won't work long term in Pre-Paid Legal," notes top producer Bill Carter. "This is about much more than just making money. It's about making a major positive impact on people's lives."

Simply stated, leadership is service, and Platinums offer the best service.

Tip #5—Prospect nonstop

"Prospecting is paramount to continued success in Pre-Paid Legal," states Paul J. Meyer. "Those who are master prospectors have more leads than they can possibly handle. When that is the case, they have a confidence that permeates their sales presentation. In addition, the percentage of sales from prospected leads is always the highest, and that is time well spent."

He concludes, "Learn how to manage your time and add in an I-will-not-be-denied attitude, combined with constant prospecting, and your becoming Platinum is inevitable!"

Tip #6—Exposures are everything

"The bottom line is that the more people you talk to, the more money you will make," notes Platinum Ed Parker.

That sums it up.

Tip #7—See yourself as staffing a company

Platinum Frank AuCoin tells a new prospect, "I don't want to presume to know where you might best fit within the company, so I will show you all the areas and let you decide which area you will be most comfortable in and that is where we will start." From there he explains the different plans that are available, the different markets, the different approaches to making sales, etc.

"I'm simply staffing a company," he states. He encourages new Associates to recruit, even if they are not comfortable with it. "It's vitally important to building a strong organization, and most people understand that," he says. "The greatest challenge is having people understand the need to develop their leadership skills, but those who want to be the leader of their company accept the challenge."

> **Platinum Advice:**
> "Will your activity get you where you want to go? If so, keep going. If not, change."
> —Nick Serba

Tip #8—Don't prejudge

Honestly speaking, what does a leader look like? "You can't prejudge in this business," says Platinum Steve Fleming. "You can't focus only on 'leaders,' because you will disqualify those who don't make your grade. That will hurt you over time."

Case in point, as Platinum Ed Parker states:

> Before I joined Pre-Paid Legal, I was in a meeting when a long-haired rock-n-roll guitar player walked in. Nobody wanted to talk to him and they took him lightly, but he went on to make more than $3,000,000 in his first four years in the business. He cut his hair, bought a suit, and became one of the biggest success stories in that company.

"Pre-Paid Legal is an incredible company with an incredible opportunity," top trainer Jeff Olson states, "but it is always comes back to the individual. Some will take advantage of the opportunity and some won't."

The sure way to never prejudge is to give everyone a chance.

The process of developing leaders

Tip #9—Be normal

One of the most commonly overlooked roadblocks to success in Pre-Paid Legal is that of forgetting to be normal," says Platinum Alan Erdlee. "New Associates often put pressure on their friends or show up unannounced on someone's doorstep. They wouldn't do that before they joined Pre-Paid Legal and they certainly shouldn't do it now!"

As a result of the awkward feelings and pressured sales presentations, the response is very poor...and as a result of the poor response, many new Associates quit.

"You must relax and be normal," Alan reiterates. "When you would want to buy from yourself or become an Associate with yourself, you know you are being normal."

Simply present the service and the opportunity, they will sell themselves.

Tip #10—Sort, don't convince

Platinum Larry Smith explains, "A while ago I asked a new recruit, 'How do you want me to respond when you are in this self-doubt phase?' We discussed it. Then the first week he hit his self-doubt phase! He got total rejection from everyone because he was trying to sell it instead of using the tools."

> **Platinum Advice:**
> "Professionals sort, amateurs convince." —*Larry Smith*

As a leader, Larry followed up with the new recruit: "You said you wanted me to schedule a follow-up meeting when you were in this self-doubt phase, so that is what I'd like to do with you."

They scheduled a meeting a couple days later, but the individual never showed up. Larry left three voice mail messages but said he would not leave any more. "I'm not in the baby-sitting business," Larry explains. "I have to spend my time with people who want to do this rather than spend my time trying to convince people that they ought to do it. Professionals sort, amateurs convince."

This principle applies to sales just as it does to prospects and recruits.

Where developing leaders will take you

Developing leaders will take you to the top. Those who buy into the process will reap the benefits. Those who are hesitant to go through the process usually get hung up on the peripheral things, like undergoing change, working outside their comfort zone, leaving their ego at the door, etc. They fail to understand, as Platinum Mike Melia outlines, that the basic steps to leadership development are also the basics of reaching Platinum:

A) Grow your team at a challenging rate, which includes new sales, new Associates, new Executive Directors, etc.

B) Continue along the path of personal growth and development.

C) Become less necessary to your team.

D) Follow the system and continue doing the fundamentals.

It is a process, but those who go through the process of developing leaders know it is worth getting it right. They have commission statements, friendships, rings, relationships, residual income, time freedom, bonuses, financial freedom, and awards to prove it. They also have leadership.

The process of developing leaders

To those who want to reach Platinum:

Platinum is really the developing of leaders—individuals who at least have a high level of commitment (going to events, weekly meetings, etc.), belief in the membership, and are disciplined to do the business.

Once you identify the leaders, I do the following 6 things with them:

1. Show them the big picture (get them to a big event).
2. Communicate regularly.
3. Pour on the recognition (plaques, etc.).
4. Sell their spouse (involve the spouse, make them feel involved, sell them on the dream-the spouse can be the best/worst support).
5. Become their friend.
6. Stay out of their way—they will develop and build without you.

Strong leaders develop close friendships and friends don't quit friends.

—Platinum Mark Riches

Part III
DEVELOPING LEADERS TO DEVELOP LEADERS

Chapter 8—*The only way to the top*

Chapter #8 reveals:

1. Where duplication begins

2. The goal of duplication

3. How to create duplication

4. 7 tips for duplication

5. The structure of duplication

Justice For All

The only way to the top
—utilizing the power of duplication

Duplication and reaching the level of Platinum go hand in hand. They are inseparable. There is not a Platinum in Pre-Paid Legal who has not utilized the power of duplication.

This simply means that to be Platinum, you must understand and use duplication to your benefit.

Why duplication?

Platinum Brian Carruthers states clearly, "You have to have duplication to get anywhere. Without it, whatever you are doing is just a treadmill."

Duplication is what allows your efforts and the efforts of your team to multiply exponentially. Duplication is what enabled Platinum David Stecki to earn more than $16,000 in one day, even though he was not the one making all those sales! Duplication is what brought in 10,000 memberships in one month to one Platinum's team!

Examples of duplication are limitless, *but would it not mean a lot more if the results of such phenomenal duplication were to your advantage?* And that is why duplication is important to everyone.

Duplication is first a mindset

How you think will obviously affect how you act. Top producer Tom Wood points out that "our philosophies affect our attitude, which in turn creates habits that produce results that lead right into our lifestyle." It looks like this:

philosophies → attitude → habits → results → lifestyle

To get the lifestyle you want, such as time freedom, financial freedom, and $16,000 days, it will require a duplication mindset. Platinums have fostered this mindset to the point that it permeates everything about them...and their lifestyle reflects it.

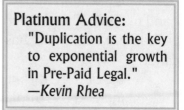

Platinum Advice:
"Duplication is the key to exponential growth in Pre-Paid Legal."
—*Kevin Rhea*

Platinum David Stecki says, "When it comes to duplication, the biggest sale is ourselves. We must have the belief system in place that prepares us to do what we need to do."

Part of that belief comes from using your Pre-Paid Legal membership, touring your local law firm, and getting to a national convention. "Those three things lock in your belief system," David states. "It helps people get a full picture of the service."

From there David explains:

You must have a strong WHY for being in the business; a WHY that is strong enough to make you cry. Whatever that reason and whatever it is you want, put it on your dream list and stick it on your office wall so you can see it regularly. Your dream list will remind you why you are in this business and refocus you when you might be having a bad day. Also, attach affirmations like "I am going to be Executive Director by X date!" and "I'm the best presenter!" Your mind doesn't know the difference between reality and fiction, so feed your mind what you want it to believe.

David concludes by saying, "The sacrifices you make along the way are just temporary. The lifestyle will be worth it in five years, so press forward through the hard times because you know where you are going."

The goal of duplication

The goal of duplication is to duplicate or replace yourself so that you can "achieve true walk-away residual income that continues to multiply with you or without you," as Platinum Mark Eldridge points out, "but replacing yourself is much easier said than done."

The only way to replace yourself, Mark explains, "is to find other people who are going to the top of the mountain with or without you. They are unstoppable and there is no question that they'll soon be Platinum if they aren't already. They have the burning passion, drive, and desire that it takes to get to the top."

Finding people takes time. Platinum Michael Dorsey notes that most of his core leadership has come from people who brought someone into the business who brought someone into the business who brought someone into the business, etc.

> **Platinum Advice:**
> "This business is all about three things: finding people to talk to, talking to the people you find, and teaching those individuals who join you to do the same. This duplicates time and time again."
> —*Michael S. Clouse*

"But even if it takes three to five years to build an empire, isn't it worth it?" Mark Eldridge asks. "The challenge is supporting your leaders enough, but not so much that they aren't growing them-

The only way to the top

selves." Platinum Antonio Adair notes from experience, "You must think 'develop' rather than 'help.' If you only help, you aren't duplicating, but you develop when you help in such a way that they learn how to do it on their own. They become stronger when they do the work…and you have duplicated yourself."

Clearly, duplication has everything to do with the leaders on your team. The goal of duplication is to not only have a walk-away income, but also to have a group of strong leaders who are doing what you are doing.

Duplicating only what duplicates

When you break it down, there is only one part of duplication that duplicates: *the people*. That is why Platinums pour their effort and energy into their leaders. With that aim, here is what the Platinums recommend:

As you start working with your team:

Start with Game Plan interview: Platinum Patrick Shaw states, "New Associates who are serious and ready for action will have their list of 100+ names completed when you meet for your Game Plan interview. If

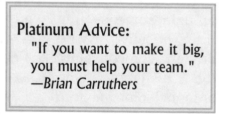

Platinum Advice:
"If you want to make it big, you must help your team."
—Brian Carruthers

they haven't completed the list, then they aren't serious or they didn't understand. I'll explain again how important it is to start with the list and we'll schedule to meet at a later date. I meet and work with only those who are serious. It's checker-

The only way to the top

board management and it starts with the Game Plan interview."

The Game Plan helps to both screen possible leaders as well as set up a "duplicatable" approach to getting started.

Use the system, use the tools—"Use the system that Pre-Paid Legal has developed to make sales and get recruits," explains Platinum Brian Carruthers, "because systems create consistency and that allows the emphasis to be on that system as opposed to any one individual." This is very good news for new Associates.

Get new Associates to Senior Associate and in Player's Club ASAP—"That combination will take you to the top," says Platinum Frank AuCoin. "Every leader should be asking, 'Who are the Associates I am working with to get to Senior Associate?'" Platinum Alan Erdlee adds, "The sooner new Associates get three recruits themselves, the sooner they can start building their team and getting to the next level."

Find the new Associates' WHY—"Not enough can be said about having a strong WHY for being in Pre-Paid Legal," says Platinum Kathy Aaron. "People will do anything, stay motivated, refuse to quit, overcome incredible odds, and more when they have a strong WHY. Everything else is immaterial."

She adds, "In addition to helping them state or establish their strong WHY, developing a personal relationship with Associates allows the duplicating process to go on to the next person. That is one way to develop duplication of strong leaders."

Train new Associates—"New Associates who aren't trained most likely won't make it," says Platinum Kelvin Collins. "Either on the phone or in person,

I accompany my new Associates to their contacts. I make the presentation and the new Associates learn, then they do it on their own."

Platinum Brian Carruthers agrees and notes, "When you train your Associates, they believe they can sell and recruit. Then when they do the same with their Associates, the selling, recruiting, and training will duplicate."

Look for leaders—Platinum Steve Fleming points out, "Leaders can be developed, but what I look for initially are people who are passionate about life and who want to become the best that they can be."

From there, Platinum Larry Smith looks for people who Fast Start qualify, attend the meetings, and plug into the activities, all the aspects of getting started right. "When I see people acting like leaders," he says, "I have a leadership Game Plan interview with them where we discuss the fact that they are CEOs of their own company, that they set the

> **Platinum Advice:**
> "Most people who get excited without adequate training will destroy their warm market."
> —*Frank AuCoin*

leadership standard for their company, etc. I help them to set 30-day goals, then have follow up meetings every 30 days to help them achieve Executive Director. During this process, they are learning how to duplicate this with their leaders."

After you have established a relationship:

Show that support is there—It is extremely important that new Associates know you are there for them. "I'm as committed to you as you are to you,"

Platinum Bill Hamilton reminds his new Associates. Platinum Mark Brown explains, "You have to help Associates through the good and bad times. That means you are working with them, supporting them, training them, etc. They need to know you'll be there for them."

Communicate—"Every morning Frank is calling his team," says Platinum Theresa AuCoin of her husband, "asking: 'How did yesterday go? Who are you seeing today? What's going on? Can we do a three-way call?' It's such a benefit to the team." Staying in contact with your team's leaders will ensure that they stay on track.

Have everyone on the same page—Because the opportunity in Pre-Paid Legal is so large, Platinum Frank AuCoin takes extra care to make sure everyone is on the same page. "You must sell the team on a unified vision of where they want to take this," he says. "Without a unified vision, without a team to pull it off, without a training of the system to get it done, without the culture, and without the events, you'll never get it done." He also knows that the size of the reward matches the size of the opportunity.

Let leaders lead: Platinum Ronnie Robinson advises, "Let new leaders present, train, speak, etc. Take yourself out of the picture as much as possible because it allows your leaders to rise up."

In addition, Platinum Steve Fleming points out, "When you

> **Platinum Advice:**
> "Do simple things with a large group of people over a long period of time."
> —*David Stecki*

find leaders and let them lead, it builds respect

within their group for their leadership, and that is key." By fanning the flame of the new leaders, Steve further motivates both the new leaders as well as the entire team. "This not only duplicates," he adds, "but it teaches duplication very nicely."

Make it impossible for the new Associate to quit— Platinum Mark Brown notes, "You want a lot of people in the business for the new Associates before they quit. Build business under them, use their prospect list, and help them recruit so they can't quit." This does not mean you do all the work, but it does mean that you come alongside them to help with their prospects, even "calling some of their prospects that they are afraid to call," says Platinum John Hoffman.

The more difficult it is for new Associates to quit, the more duplication you have taking place on your team.

While working long-term as a team:

Don't be their boss—Platinum Larry King states, "You can't boss a leader; you either lead, follow, or get out of the way."

Keep it simple—"Anything that you want to duplicate must be kept simple," notes top trainer Jeff Olson, "and that is the hard part." The answer is to always go back to the basics of daily exposures, presentations, PBRs, etc. and to never do anything more complex than the basics.

Spend time with the top people—"To get to Platinum, you have to spend your best time with the right people," says Platinum Brian Carruthers. "Spending time with the right people who are making it happen will make your time well spent.

For example, the person who wants to move from $8,000 a month to $16,000 a month is where you need to be spending the bulk of your time."

With these top people, however, there is a limit to how much you can do. Brian points out, "Teach the top

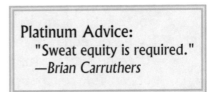

Platinum Advice:
"Sweat equity is required."
—Brian Carruthers

producers everything you can teach them, then get out of their way. Become their colleague and friend and let them develop into the leaders they need to become."

Set high standards—"I aim to double my leaders' production and organization every quarter," says Platinum KC Townes. "We set goals and work together to reach those goals, but I only work with those who are actively working towards their goals." In short, plan your work and work your plan, then teach your team to do the same

Work as a team—Everyone benefits when the entire team is taking the same steps. Platinum Mike Melia teaches his leaders to create duplication by sticking to these basics at all times:
1) follow and promote the 10 Core Commitments,
2) provide/facilitate a weekly leadership call and give upcoming leaders the spotlight,
3) identify potential leaders ASAP and "take them under your wing,"
4) treat people with respect, and
5) provide breakout sessions at all major events and run events around the events, such as cruises, houseboat trips, rafting expeditions, etc.

Inspect and expect duplication—"I have given support to those I recruited and I tell them that I

The only way to the top

expect them to give the same support to the people they recruit," states Platinum Bill Hamilton. "However, I let people know that, regardless of level, if they need support from their leader and don't get it, I am available." Occasionally he will have someone call who is not being supported. After he hangs up, he then contacts whoever is responsible for that person and finds out just why what he is saying is not reaching to the whole team. "That is how I inspect what I expect," Bill explains.

Tips for duplication

As you know, hindsight is always 20/20, and that is especially good when it comes to duplication. Here are the top 7 tips from the Platinums for making duplication work for you and your team:

Tip #1—Use an expert

Nobody wants to be rejected by family and friends, but for most new Associates, their warm market is their family and friends. Instead of ignoring their warm market, the answer is to use an expert, which can be a Pre-Paid Legal video or audio that explains the service or another Associate who can do the talking.

> **Platinum Advice:**
> "Until you are making more money than the guy at the top, stick with what's proven." —*Darrin Kidd*

Using an expert is the best route for two reasons: 1) if the prospects hate it, they hate the expert, and 2) using an expert is highly "duplicatable." Either way you win when you use an expert.

Tip #2—Get referrals and name lists

Paul J. Meyer always states, "I'd rather be a master prospector than a wizard of speech and have no one to tell my story to." A master prospector will have more names to contact than there are hours in a day, and that is a very good position to be in. Also, the sale ratio of a referral from a warm market is always better than that of cold calls. "Always ask for referrals," Platinum Patrick Shaw states, "always!"

Platinum Dan Stammen, when he recruits someone, makes it a point to put together a prospect list with his new recruit and then to get a copy of that list. He tells the new recruit:

> I'd like to keep a copy of this list, and here's why: I'm full-time, you're part-time and just getting started. You understand that I'm not going to pressure anyone to sign up. All I want to do is get some information in their hands so they can view a live presentation or some third-party documentation. We'll go from there. I'd like to keep a copy of this list so that tomorrow while you are at work I can make some of these calls myself.

Dan adds, "I know the #1 thing that will keep new Associates going in the business is having some success underneath them." Also, as top trainer Jeff Olson points out, "You will have more power in their list of 100 names than you will in your own

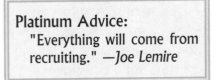

Platinum Advice:
"Everything will come from recruiting." —*Joe Lemire*

list." Working together with a person's leads is always a smart move.

The only way to the top

Tip #3—Don't slow down

"The incredible opportunity of Pre-Paid Legal is available to everyone," says Platinum David Stecki. "There are millions of people who want the service and the company is perfectly poised for massive growth, but not everyone is going to take advantage of the opportunity. Instead of slowing down for people who criticize you, who don't like the service, or complain about having to work, just move on!"

It is all about keeping your attitude up and moving forward.

Tip #4—Work with prospects, not suspects

Platinum Nick Serba says, "Prospects are people who fit your paradigm: they are looking for extra income, they have the need, you can help meet it, etc. Most Associates spend a lot of time trying to recruit the same people, convincing them that they need to become Associates. These people are suspects, not prospects."

The answer is to "spend enough time so that they understand, then let them go," explains Nick. Whether you are trying to make a membership sale or gain a recruit, look for prospects and leave the suspects alone.

Platinum Mark Riches takes this approach: "I ask prospects, 'On scale from 1-10, with 1 being that you are window shopping and 10 being that you are ready to get started, where would you rate yourself?' If they are 6 and below, I say, 'I'm looking for people who are more interested. When you are, let me know.' You need to become a sorter, not a convincer."

Tip #5—Keep it simple

If something is simple, anyone can do it. "The average person is the one who is going to make the most sales," says Platinum Fran Alexander, "so keeping it simple, from presenting the service to recruiting others, allows everyone to do it." Top trainer Jeff Olson always says, "Whatever you do in Pre-Paid Legal, it has to work four or five levels below you, 2000 miles away, without you present, with a dud talking to a stud." That is the essence of simplicity.

Tip #6—Spend time with your recruits

"When new Associates start, their anxiety level is high but their knowledge level is low," notes Platinum Patrick Shaw. "The secret is to spend considerable time with new Associates, helping, training, and encouraging."

Platinum Nick Serba agrees, "You should spend a little bit of time recruiting a few people, then spend a lot of time with those few people that you've recruited."

The more training, the more success. For example, those who attend the Fast Start classes have on average much higher levels of success than do those who do not. Taking the time with your recruits to increase their level of knowledge will substantially decrease Associates' anxiety, and that will mean more sales, more recruits, and more growth to your team. Top trainer Eric Worre sums it up when he says, "Slow down to go fast."

Tip #7—Lead by example

Platinum Brian Carruthers says, "You have to be leading by example. Occasionally you will have someone on your team who will do more than you, but 99.9% of your recruits will do what you are doing or less."

If you are doing what Platinum Dave Savula recommends of "two exposures a day and attending a weekly meeting," your team will follow your lead. If you do more, they will follow that as well.

"Our tendency is to tell, tell, tell, tell, like a boss," adds Platinum Darrin Kidd. "Instead, it needs to be tell, show, try, and do—tell new Associates what to do, show them how to do it, let them try it, then they do it." This is one of the best ways to make sure that everyone is on the same page...and duplicating!

The structure of duplication

Duplication is focused, orderly, and intentional. It has structure. If it were not structured, it would be chaotic and destined for failure. That is why Platinums take the structure of duplication so seriously. "Without structure, you are spinning your wheels, expending unnecessary effort," states Platinum Kevin Rhea.

To reach the level of Platinum, you need four solid Executive Director legs. National Marketing Director of Pre-Paid Legal and Platinum, Wilburn Smith, notes, "I was taught to build five Associates wide and three Associates deep. I've never been able to prove that wrong." And because not every frontline recruit will become a top producer, as Platinum Nick Serba points out, "You may need four to six Associates frontline to get the three you need."

From Senior Associate to Executive Director to Platinum, those who are serious about Pre-Paid Legal know exactly where they are, which leg they need to work with, and where they are going. Platinum Steve Fleming advises, "Instead of having a goal of when you want to reach Platinum, write down when you want your leaders to reach Platinum. If that is your goal, you'll be Platinum anyway, since they will reach Executive Director on the way to Platinum."

With your structure, you ideally want to recruit up, getting better and better recruits as you go. "Bring in your sharpest people," recommends Platinum Joe Lemire. "Not only is that wise, but it keeps you from slipping back. I look for five potential Platinums in my team, just as we teach our team to work on their five Director lines. Having five strong legs will cover you

The only way to the top

during the slow times and keep you from slipping off of your present level."

Platinums Frank and Theresa AuCoin agree, "You don't want to make Platinum and fall out. You need successful leaders below you, Executive Directors who are making 10k a month. Under those four leaders you at least want six people who are also at the Executive Director level. That will bring stability to the whole group."

> **Platinum Advice:**
> "The common denominator for success is action. Without action you lose vision, confidence, and determination to achieve."
> —*Kevin Rhea*

"We continue to work in a leg until it's solid with six Executive Directors in it," adds Theresa. "One wreck, stroke, death, or accident can take out an entire leg. We teach our team to keep developing until the leg is solid, and that means as many as 25 meetings (PBRs, trainings, luncheons, etc.) going on each week per leg."

Every Platinum wants long-term, walk-away income. With stability and security, it will happen...*and it already has happened.*

Two final keys to duplication

At its core, duplication is bound up in one word: *action.* Action is what drives everything, for without action, there would be no duplication. Action produces knowledge and experience, which in turn produce self-confidence. "Self-confidence is the key to all achievement," notes Paul J. Meyer, "but most Associates don't follow the necessary steps to get the self-confidence they so desperately need to excel in Pre-Paid Legal."

Here is the sequence:

1) *self-confidence* is gained through practical *know-how*

2) *know-how* comes from *knowledge and experience*

3) *knowledge and experience* come through *action*

It is simple: those who gain the necessary self-confidence also gain the money, as action produces both.

Duplication is also directly related to your vision. "You must have a vision of where you want to take this," advises Platinum Frank AuCoin, "because a motivating vision is required to have people follow you. They will buy into your vision because your vision is bigger than their own vision. Without a vision, everything comes to a screeching halt. Duplication always requires vision."

When you have a vision that moves you to action, you are on track to the top, and duplication will follow.

To those who want to reach Platinum:

1. Allow yourself to dream.
2. Translate your dreams into goals with a plan.
3. Set your goals, prepare, and then launch, without expecting immediate success.
4. Take one step at a time and recruit one Associate at a time.
5. Watch out for dream-stealers.
6. Develop resilience and persist in the face of failure.
7. Try, try again, try another way, and never, never give up.

—Platinum Steve Fleming

The only way to the top

Part III
DEVELOPING LEADERS TO DEVELOP LEADERS

Chapter 9—*Moving beyond Platinum*

Chapter #9 reveals:

1. How to maintain and move beyond Platinum

2. Staying focused on the basics

3. The power of forward momentum

4. Why Platinums focus on stability

5. What comes after Platinum

Justice For All

Moving beyond Platinum
—what to do when you hit the top

"The ultimate pinnacle in Pre-Paid Legal is reaching the level of Platinum," says Platinum Brian Carruthers. "It shows you are a master at building the business, that you are a master at building other people, and that you have mastered the art of duplication. It means that you have a lifestyle and an income that most will just dream about."

Brian adds, "It also means that *your work has just begun!*"

What happens when you reach Platinum?

When you reach Platinum, two goals become immediately obvious:

#1—to maintain the level of Platinum

#2—to move up to Platinum 2, 3, and beyond

Both goals are of utmost importance to everyone who reaches this prestigious level, but what are the requirements? What must you do to maintain the level of Platinum while at the same time move up to the next level? "The way to reach Platinum is the same way to remain at Platinum," notes Platinum Antonio Adair. "*It is also the same way to move beyond Platinum.*"

In short, the two goals are one in the same.

"The answer is to keep doing what worked to get you there in the first place," Platinums Ed and Patti Parker explain. "When we hit Platinum our 11th month in the business, we tried to do things differently...and things stagnated as a result."

But as every Platinum is quick to recognize what works and what does not, the Parkers point out, "We immediately changed back to what makes it work from the very beginning levels and business picked up speed again."

> **Platinum Advice:**
> "Never be content. It doesn't stop at Platinum."
> —Antonio Adair

So just what does it take, practically speaking, to maintain and to move up? Here is what the Platinums advise:

● **Stick with the basics**

The basics of Pre-Paid Legal always revolve around sales and recruiting. "Massive exposure and lots of tools, those are the basics," says Platinum Mark Riches.

Platinum Frank AuCoin notes, "All it takes for success in Pre-Paid Legal is consistent exposure of the member benefits and business opportunity to one, two, or three people a day, depending on your goals, and attending the training meetings."

Platinum Antonio Adair adds, "The answer is to stay in Phase #1, do the 10 Core Commitments, don't get into management mode, and keep going." Excellent advice, considering the fact that the basics are all about taking action, and action is what makes money in Pre-Paid Legal. Action is also solely responsible for people reaching the level of Platinum.

● **Maintain forward momentum**

Momentum will come automatically from repetitive action over a period of time. "Once you create momentum, you don't want to lose it," states Platinum Darnell Self.

How true, but what do Platinums do to maintain the momentum? In brief, they simply keep doing what they have been doing. "Momentum has a life of its own," says Platinum Kevin Rhea, "sweeping everyone along, creating an even bigger wave of excitement, vision, and action."

But strangely enough, some people pull the plug on their momentum just as it starts to pick up speed. "They let the momentum die because they think it could end at any moment," explains Platinum Mark Brown. Others let the air out

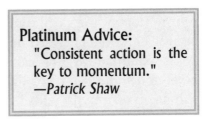

Platinum Advice:
"Consistent action is the key to momentum."
—*Patrick Shaw*

of their momentum because they get off track, get busy with something else, or become discouraged by someone's negative comment.

Whatever the reason, there is no excuse worth losing your momentum!

● *Keep the excitement and enthusiasm*

"I've been in Pre-Paid Legal a long time," says Platinum Ken Moore, who was one of the first Associates within the company, "and after all these years, I wake up excited about Pre-Paid Legal every day. I get tired like everyone else, but I'm excited about this service and opportunity."

He points out, "I've been sick many times since we've started, twice I was told I wouldn't live, and all the while my residual income was there! What's more, a friend of mine who was completely broke when he started in Pre-Paid Legal recently put his house on the market for $1.5 million! Pre-Paid Legal is an incredible company."

Platinum Steve Melia says, "Excitement is reward enough for people. I can't count the number of new Associates I've seen who are walking with a bounce in their step again—it's as if they have a new lease on life. It may take a little longer to see the financial return, depending on the individual and past experience, but the emotional reward up front is most important."

> **Platinum Advice:**
> "Take the relationship with your leaders dead seriously."
> —Frank AuCoin

Maintaining that excitement and enthusiasm is the goal, and though part of that is answered in the relationships you form with your team, the majority of excitement and enthusiasm is internal, self-motivated. That is why Platinums have plenty of excitement and enthusiasm to share with others.

- *Cultivate friendships that last a lifetime*
  "The money is obviously good, but it's really all about friendships," states Platinum Ed Parker. "You are literally forming friendships that will last a lifetime, which is of value and benefit to everyone. To do that, people need to know that you care and that you are genuinely interested in them. As the friendship grows, so will your team."

Platinum Theresa AuCoin adds, "The relationships in your team is what will hold your team together. If you are serious about your business, then build the team by caring about those on your team, keeping in regular contact with them, being available to help them, and recognizing them for their achievements every chance you get."

As is expected, all Platinums have close friendships within their teams. To not have that type of friendship and be Platinum is impossible.

Moving beyond Platinum

- *Stay disciplined*

   Just as Pre-Paid Legal pays daily, so Platinums take action on a daily basis. Platinum Michael Dorsey says, "I know every day what I need to do that day: how many calls to make, how many tapes to get out, how many people to contact, the trainings, one-on-ones, conferences, etc. I know what I need to do weekly and monthly, and I do it daily."

   It takes discipline to reach, maintain, and move beyond Platinum.

   Platinum Brian Carruthers notes, "Jim Rohn always says, 'Daily discipline is what bridges the gap between your dreams and reality.' I couldn't agree more. Discipline is what separates the dreamers from the achievers, but what is interesting is that discipline falls right in line for those who have a strong WHY and a big vision."

> **Platinum Advice:**
> "Don't slip back. Once you hit Platinum, keep going forward." —*Antonio Adair*

- *Focus on stability*

   Stability is extremely important at the Platinum level. According to the Platinums, stability includes:

   Developing leaders—Platinum Antonio Adair candidly admits, "At one time I had five Executive Directors in one leg within our organization, some of which had even hit Silver Executive Director and were making $16,000 a month. I felt secure about that team, but it fell completely apart. The leaders needed to be developed, not helped."

   Platinum Mark Riches explains, "An Associate needs to create a Senior Associate

169

factory while a Platinum needs to create a leadership factory. You can't get to the top with a handful of leaders—you need to develop 15-20 good leaders. The goal is to develop more leaders faster."

Helping others—"Stability is money in this industry," says Platinum Larry Smith. "I'll help anyone at any level within my team as that is beneficial to them and to me. I'll also work with someone who isn't even in my organization because I recognize that if I can help stabilize someone else's team, it will help stabilize mine."

Making sales and recruiting all the time—Telling is not good enough. "You must always lead by example," advises Platinum David Stecki. "Keep out of the management mode. Recruit and market memberships constantly, because people do what you do, not what you say." Consistent sales through a team means stability at every level, and that is what Platinums aim for.

Maintaining high persistency—For every Associate, especially those who are Platinum, the residual income from membership sales is the real prize. Paul J. Meyer notes, "You can make a sale today, and though you

> **Platinum Advice:**
> "Keep doing what you did to get there." —*Darnell Self*

enjoy the advanced commissions right then and there, being able to draw a residual commission on that same sale for the next 10 to 20 years or longer is incredible!"

To maximize your residual income, persistency must remain high, which is why Platinum Mark Brown highly recommends utilizing the services of Integrity Resource Management (www.integrity4you.com).

"Having Integrity Resources write letters and make phone calls to new members for the first 12 months of their membership is a great way to retain members," Mark explains, *"and membership retention is everything!* The cost is minute in comparison to what you both save and gain. Everyone who thinks long term in Pre-Paid Legal does what it takes to keep their persistency high."

- *Be balanced*

Some say it is a sprint to Platinum and others say it is a marathon. However you see it, reaching Platinum is not the finish line. "It's just the beginning," says Platinum Antonio Adair. So whether you run fast or run slow, make sure you run strong so that you can continue toward even greater success. That is what balance is all about.

Another important aspect of balance, as Platinum David Stecki notes, "is that you learn how to juggle between producing and helping others produce. Your team needs you and you need to lead by example."

Clearly, balance is not the easiest thing in the world to gain. It comes with experience, learning what to do and what not to do. Platinum John Hoffman explains, "Balance is critical. I didn't always have balance and was heading down the road to losing my wife and kids. If my own family is out of order, how can I teach someone about success? Balance is critical."

171

Keep your perspective of what is most important in life.

After reaching Platinum, what's next?

The lifestyle that Platinums enjoy enables them to "do anything you want, making decisions based on what you want to do rather than on financial limitations," say Platinums Steve and Kim Melia.

> **Platinum Advice:**
> "Whether it takes you six months or six years, reaching Platinum is all about staying in the race and finishing."
> —*Russell Peden*

"When you make a lot of money, you can also help a lot of people," National Marketing Director of Pre-Paid Legal and Platinum, Wilburn Smith, points out. "That is the fun part. I could retire, but why would I want to?"

Platinum Kevin Rhea agrees, "We put 50% of what we make from Pre-Paid Legal into a foundation that supports many of the charities and programs in our area in Texas. That is very satisfying."

"Outside of money, the reward I enjoy the most is seeing people become more than they were," says Platinum Patrick Shaw. "I always used to hear, 'It's not what you make, it's who you become that counts,' and I have come to realize that it is true."

Patrick continues, "If you said to someone who has succeeded in Pre-Paid Legal, 'You can keep your knowledge that you've gained in this process or you can keep your check, which will it be?' *without a doubt they will keep the knowledge because they have what it takes to simply turn around and replicate what they have already accomplished.*"

Platinum John Hoffman explains, "Watching people go through this growth process is a joy. Sure it takes time and effort, but the end result could never be measured in dollars."

Clearly, there are big payoffs at the Platinum level, but what do top producers actually do when they reach Platinum? They do the following:

- *Platinums speed up*
"Platinum is not the checkered flag. It's not the end. It's just a pit stop," explains Platinum Darnell Self. "You are ready to go even faster now. It's time to turn it up."

Platinums know from experience that if you slow down, the team will slow down. Darnell notes, "Today's success hurts tomorrow's success, which simply means it's human nature to ease off the pedal when you reach your goal. Don't let that happen to you!

> **Platinum Advice:**
> "When you've become Platinum:
> 1. develop other Platinums
> 2. develop ring earners
> 3. maximize persistency
> 4. develop leaders (so you work yourself out of a job)."
> —*Bill Hamilton*

At Platinum you are paid an incredible amount for what you've always done. When Tracy and I hit Platinum, our income really took off. Do NOT slow down!"

National Marketing Director of Pre-Paid Legal and Platinum, Wilburn Smith, states, "A lot of people succeeding in Pre-Paid Legal are making more money than they ever dreamed possible, and there is nothing wrong with that. However, it is very tempting to go on cruise control when you get satisfied, and that is when you get in trouble."

Platinum Fran Alexander adds, "Just because you reach Platinum doesn't mean you can quit." The coasting, the slowing down, the easing off on the pedal, and even the quitting is the result of too small a vision, explains Platinum John Gardner. "You need a vision that is bigger than yourself, far bigger!"

- *Platinums dream bigger dreams*

"The fact of the matter is," Platinum Brian Carruthers notes, "there will only be a few driven people who will hit 30, 40, 50 thousand a month and keep going. Most will get complacent and slow down, many stopping at around $10,000 a month. That is who they are and what they want to be, and that is one of the reasons why you need to keep looking for more leaders, more goal achievers, and more people who are driven to aim even higher."

Platinum Antonio Adair agrees. "It's natural for your WHY to change as you grow," he says. "The secret is to get new goals so you stay hungry, driven, and motivated." Platinum Mark Riches advises, "When you reach Platinum, keep building."

Internalizing the concept that reaching Platinum is "only the beginning" is very important. "When you can do anything you want," Platinum David Stecki points out, "it changes things considerably. I was able to go on a six-week honeymoon when I got married, but most people wouldn't have even thought about it because they couldn't have afforded it. When you have time freedom and financial freedom, everything changes."

Start dreaming bigger dreams now.

- *Platinums focus on leaving a legacy*

Platinum John Hoffman states, "What we do in the next three years affects our next 40!" Most people will not pause long enough to even consider where they will be 5,

10, or 20 years down they road. In Pre-Paid Legal, however, the opportunity exists for every Associate to create a book of business from membership sales that produces a residual income for generations to come.

"When you step away, business keeps going," says Platinum Darnell Self. "That is what you want. I intend to build the business so that it lasts for a lifetime."

> **Platinum Advice:**
> "To take it to the next level, having Platinums on your team is the next goal." —*Brian Carruthers*

Such a mindset is very uncommon. Platinum Mark Brown points out, "When people invest in a traditional business, they see it as long term, but when people start with Pre-Paid Legal, many don't take it seriously. They have a 'lottery' mentality instead of a 'business' mentality and this is to their disadvantage."

He adds, "I take it very seriously. This is no different than me opening 40 businesses that are succeeding. I plan to leave this for my family."

Platinums think long term.

- *Platinums reach Platinum again!*

"When you reach Platinum, make it your goal to reach Platinum again," says Platinum Kevin Rhea. "Having the additional Executive Director legs will strengthen both your income and your position."

Platinum Kathy Aaron notes, "As Platinum, develop as many Executive Directors and ring earners as you can. It is a sign that those leaders have reached an income level that has sustained them long term, and that is good for the whole team."

The next step is then to develop other Platinums within your team. "That is where things reach a whole

Moving beyond Platinum

new level," Platinum Brian Carruthers points out, "but you must remember that when all is said and done, Platinums continue to do what they've always done. They never get 'too cool' to sit in the front row of meetings or trainings, to be on conference calls, to do PBR presentations, to recruit, to prospect, to sell a membership, to do Game Plan Interviews, or to develop new leaders. They keep doing the same things that got them to Executive Director and then to Platinum...and they repeat the process again...and again...and again."

That is what you do when you reach the top.

To those who want to reach Platinum:

Platinum is a journey, not a destination. You'll learn many things along the way and will still be learning once you reach the level of Platinum. This really is about personal development.

If you have the passion to reach Platinum, are laser focused, and use the strategy of getting your leaders driving the 10 Core Commitments down through the depth of their teams, then it's undeniable that you'll be Platinum.

—Platinum Mark Eldridge

Conclusion

Every Associate in Pre-Paid Legal begins on the pathway to Platinum. "There really is only one path," states Platinum Brian Carruthers. "Those who make it to Platinum have stayed on track, continuing to make the sales and recruits necessary to reach the next level, and helping others within their team to do the same."

As you follow the Platinums who have gone down the path ahead of you, it is not a question of "if" you will make it to Platinum but "when."

Here's to you—congratulations!

Reference information for Pre-Paid Legal

- *Pre-Paid Legal Services, Inc.*
  PO Box 1379 Ada, OK 74821 (*new business and resubmitted or returned business*)
  PO Box 2629 Ada, OK 74821 or fax: 580-436-7496 (*bank changes and membership reinstatements*)
  PO Box 145 Ada, OK 74821 (*miscellaneous*)
  PPL Corporate Web Site: www.prepaidlegal.com

- *Marketing:*
  Marketing Services (*for all your business questions*): 580-436-7424
  Marketing Services fax: 580-436-7496
  Marketing Services email: marketingservices@pplsi.com
  Licensing questions: 580-436-7424 or licensing@pplsi.com
  Corporate Communications Fax (*for ad approvals*): 580-421-6305
  Stock Information: 800-654-7757, Option 3

- *Customer Care Services:*
  Customer Care (*membership questions*): 800-654-7757
  Customer Care Fax (*member bank & address changes*): 580-436-7565
  Legal Shield (*in case of detainment*): 877-825-3797 (toll-free)

- *Group Marketing:*
  PO Box 2479, Ada, OK 74820
  Group Questions (*Incl. Group Seminar & Small Business Seminar registration*): 580-421-6326, fax (*for questions and/or seminar registration*): 580-421-6311

Group Marketing email: groupmarketing@pplsi.com
Group Marketing conference call (*every Monday 9
a.m. EST*): 412-858-5200 or 888-379-9511)

- *Small Business Support Center:*
  866.467.6249 or www.pplbizplan.com

- *PPL Interactive Voice Response (IVR) System:*
  Call 800-699-9004, enter your Associate number and
  PIN#, then choose from the following options:
    Option 1—Recent updates
    Option 2—Main Menu
      Push 1 for Associate information
      Push 2 for Fax-on-Demand
      Push 3 for Web Support

- *Supply orders:*
  Marketing services: phone orders: 580-436-7424
    (option 3), fax orders: 580-436-7496
  Video*Plus* orders & information: 800-388-3884, fax
    orders: 940-497-9799
  Video*Plus* orders online: www.ppltools-videoplus.com

- *Communication:*
  Televox Voice Response System customer service:
    888-871-4950, fax: 888-266-6897, www.televox.cc/ppl

- *Member Retention Services:*
  Integrity Resource Management: 888-272-0986 or
    www.integrity4you.com

- *Overnight Delivery:*
  Overnight (FedEx and UPS only) to: 321 East Main Street, Ada, OK 74821
  To open a FedEx account (free), order pre-printed labels & envelopes, request pickup, track shipments: phone 800-GO-FEDEX (800-463-3339) or online at: www.fedex.com
  To open a UPS account (free), order pre-printed labels & envelopes, request pickup, track shipments: phone 800-PICK-UPS (800-742-5877) or online at: www.ups.com

- *Business Card and Letterhead*
  1) PPL Marketing Services: 321 E. Main Ada, OK 74820 or 580-436-7424
  2) Personal Image Concepts: P.O. Box 30119, Portland, OR 97294-3119 or 503-546-4191, toll-free 877-712-7712, or http://www.piconcepts.com/ppl
  3) JFA Printing: 866-532-6654 (toll free) or www.jfaonline.com
  4) The Print Centre: #108, 19915-64 Avenue Langley, BC V2Y 1G9 Canada or 604-533-2636, fax: 604-533-6552
  (NOTE: All business cards must be purchased from one of the above mentioned licensed vendors.)

- *Apparel*
  Kerma's Kreations: 800-757-1193 or www.kermas.com
  Freedom Team: 816-455-2108 or www.freedomteam.biz

- *Audios, Videos, and Presentation tools:*
  Video*Plus*: 800-388-3884 or www.ppltools-videoplus.com

- *Banners and Signs:*
  Fast Signs: 405-942-0317 or www.pplfastsigns.com

- *Presentation Boards:*
  JB's Presentations: 219-661-9260 or www.golikeapro.com

- *Badges, Trophies, and Statues:*
  Justice Galleries: 417-882-7927 or 888-882-7927
  Trophies & More: 740-383-1945

About the authors

Brian Mast, formerly the managing editor for a business magazine, is an editor, writer, and author of numerous books, including *How to Manage One Million Dollars or Less*, *Profiles of Success*, and *Success in Pre-Paid Legal*. He is also an active Pre-Paid Legal Associate.

Kevin Rhea is a Platinum and President of L-K Marketing Group, one of the leading organizations in Pre-Paid Legal. Kevin is responsible for managing and overseeing the day-to-day operations, growth, stability, and future progress of L-K Marketing. He and the leaders of L-K Marketing have put together an impressive track record of success in Pre-Paid Legal.

L-K Marketing has been recognized as a $1 Million Income Earner. Kevin is quick to point out that the credit goes directly to the many top producers in L-K Marketing. What really motivates Kevin is seeing the leaders on the team achieve their goals and receive recognition for their success in Pre-Paid Legal.

Brian Carruthers was a successful real estate agent prior to entering the network marketing arena. After moderate success in his first two endeavors in the industry, Brian leveraged the valuable knowledge gained from his experience and was ready when the Pre-Paid Legal opportunity presented itself. Brian quickly broke company records and was the quickest ever to hit Platinum. He also still holds the distinction of being the fastest (less than three years) and youngest person to achieve the Million Dollar Club.

Brian attributes his success to his non-negotiable attitude about his business and to his team of leaders who lead by example and follow the system. He acknowledges that this is all a team effort and he appreciates all of the great people who work every day toward their goals.

Brian has been featured in *Home Business Connection Magazine*, *Upline Magazine*, and *Networking Times*.

The Success in Pre-Paid Legal Series

Volume I—Success in Pre-Paid Legal

Success in Pre-Paid Legal prepares new Associates for phenomenal success with:

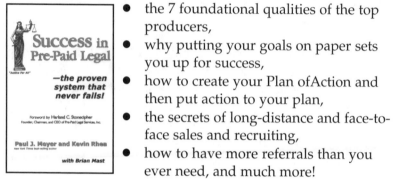

- the 7 foundational qualities of the top producers,
- why putting your goals on paper sets you up for success,
- how to create your Plan of Action and then put action to your plan,
- the secrets of long-distance and face-to-face sales and recruiting,
- how to have more referrals than you ever need, and much more!

Packed with advice and insights from 30 of Pre-Paid Legal's top producers and top trainers, *Success in Pre-Paid Legal* is where new Associates begin.

"This is a must-read for every new Associate." –Platinum Kevin Rhea

Volume II—Pathway to Platinum

Pathway to Platinum walks tomorrow's leaders in Pre-Paid Legal through the steps necessary to reach the prestigious

level of Platinum, including:

- the 12 keys to reaching Platinum,
- setting the pace for unstoppable momentum,
- how to develop leaders on your team,
- the ins and outs of leading a successful team,
- what you do when you hit the top, and much more!

More than 50 Platinums, top producers, and top trainers in Pre-Paid Legal explain exactly how to reach the top.

"Anyone who is serious about reaching Platinum needs to read this book—more than once!" —Platinum Brian Carruthers

To order more copies of *Success in Pre-Paid Legal* and *Pathway to Platinum* from Video*Plus*:

- Online: <u>www.ppltools-videoplus.com</u>
- Phone: 800-388-3884
- Fax: 940-497-9799
- Mail: Video*Plus* Inc. 200 Swisher Road Lake, Dallas, TX 75065
  (*Single copies and bulk orders are available.*)

Notes:

Notes:

<u>Notes</u>:

Notes:

Notes:

Notes:

Notes:

Puppy or Kitten?

EVEN MORE
QUICK QUIZZES FOR BFFs

For Norman, my favorite kitty.

—S.H.

ISBN 978-0-545-28441-7

12 11 10 9 8 7 6 5 4 3   11 12 13 14 15/0

Printed in the U.S.A.   40

First printing, September 2010

Illustrations and book design by Janet Kusmierski

PuppY or Kitten?

EVEN MORE QUICK QUIZZES FOR BFFs

BY SIERRA HARIMANN

SCHOLASTIC INC.

New York   Toronto   London   Auckland

Sydney   Mexico City   New Delhi   Hong Kong

Are you neat and organized or a total slob?

Do you text during movies?

Is a girl's best friend a puppy or a kitten?

Would you rather sing karaoke or make up a dance routine?

How well do you know your BFF?

Take these quizzes with your friends, and then compare your answers.

HAVE A BLAST!

Remarkable Room!

What does your space say about you?

1. Do you ⬤ Share a room or ◯ Have your own space?

2. Who chose the décor? ◯ Me ◯ My sibling or ◯ My parents

3. The color scheme in my room is *purpal an green*

4. Is your room ◯ Really girly and pink or ◯ Not feminine at all?

5. If you hung an animal poster on your wall, would it be a
   ◯ Puppy or ◯ Kitten?

6. Do you like posters of ◯ Celebrities
   ◯ Animals or ◯ Bands?

7. ◯ Painted walls or ◯ Wallpaper?

8. ◯ Glow-in-the-dark sticker stars or
   ◯ Blue sky and fluffy white clouds?

9. Are your siblings allowed in your room? ◯ Sure ◯ Only
   if they knock first or ◯ Absolutely not!

10. Is your room ◯ Neat and organized ◯ A total pigsty or
    ◯ It depends on my mood?

11. Do you clean your room ◯ Once a week ◯ Once a month or
    ◯ Only when my parents make me?

12. ◯ A TV in your room or ◯ No such luck?

13. Do you ◯ Have your own computer or ◯ Have to share?

14. When you call your friends, do you use ◯ Your cell phone
    ◯ Your bedroom phone or ◯ The house phone?

15. Do you write in a ◯ Journal ◯ Diary or ◯ Blog?

16. What's more important to you: ◯ Phone ◯ TV or ◯ Computer?

17. ◯ Your favorite TV show or ◯ A great movie?

18. Do your homework ◯ At your desk ◯ On your bed or ◯ Somewhere else in the house?

19. ◯ Your own bathroom or ◯ I wish!?

20. ◯ Top bunk or ◯ Bottom bunk?

21. ◯ Twin-size bed or ◯ Full-size bed?

22. ◯ Lots of pillows or ◯ Only one?

23. Before bed, do you ◯ Read ◯ Listen to music or ◯ Watch TV?

24. Are you ◯ An early bird or ◯ A night owl?

25. When you sleep, do you ◯ Leave the door open ◯ Open it a crack or ◯ It's got to be closed?

26. Do you sleep on your ◯ Stomach ◯ Side or ◯ Back?

27. Do you snore? ◯ Yes ◯ No or ◯ How would I know?

28. Do you sleep with a stuffed animal or special blanket? ◯ No way! ◯ Yes, and it's no big deal or ◯ I'll never admit it even if I do!

29. Do you use a night-light? ◯ Are you kidding? ◯ Um yeah, but don't tell!

30. ◯ Alarm clock or ◯ My parents wake me up?

Remarkable Room!

What does your space say about you?

1. Do you ⦾ Share a room or ◯ Have your own space?

2. Who chose the décor? ◯ Me ◯ My sibling or ⦾ My parents

3. The color scheme in my room is __blue__.

4. Is your room ◯ Really girly and pink or ⦾ Not feminine at all?

5. If you hung an animal poster on your wall, would it be a

   ⦾ Puppy or ◯ Kitten?

6. Do you like posters of ◯ Celebrities

   ⦾ Animals or ◯ Bands?

7. ⦾ Painted walls or ◯ Wallpaper?

8. ⦾ Glow-in-the-dark sticker stars or

   ◯ Blue sky and fluffy white clouds?

9. Are your siblings allowed in your room? ◯ Sure ◯ Only

   if they knock first or ⦾ Absolutely not!

10. Is your room ◯ Neat and organized ◯ A total pigsty or

    ⦾ It depends on my mood?

11. Do you clean your room ◯ Once a week ◯ Once a month or

    ⦾ Only when my parents make me?

12. ◯ A TV in your room or ⦾ No such luck?

13. Do you ◯ Have your own computer or ⦾ Have to share?

14. When you call your friends, do you use ◯ Your cell phone

    ◯ Your bedroom phone or ⦾ The house phone?

15. Do you write in a ⦾ Journal ◯ Diary or ◯ Blog?

16. What's more important to you: ⊗ Phone ○ TV or ○ Computer?

17. ○ Your favorite TV show or ⊗ A great movie?

18. Do your homework ○ At your desk ⊗ On your bed or ○ Somewhere else in the house?

19. ○ Your own bathroom or ⊗ I wish!?

20. ○ Top bunk or ⊗ Bottom bunk?

21. ○ Twin-size bed or ⊗ Full-size bed?

22. ⊗ Lots of pillows or ○ Only one?

23. Before bed, do you ○ Read ○ Listen to music or ⊗ Watch TV?

24. Are you ○ An early bird or ⊗ A night owl?

25. When you sleep, do you ○ Leave the door open ⊗ Open it a crack or ○ It's got to be closed?

26. Do you sleep on your ⊗ Stomach ○ Side or ○ Back?

27. Do you snore? ○ Yes ○ No or ⊗ How would I know?

28. Do you sleep with a stuffed animal or special blanket? ○ No way! ⊗ Yes, and it's no big deal or ○ I'll never admit it even if I do!

29. Do you use a night-light? ⊗ Are you kidding? ○ Um yeah, but don't tell!

30. ⊗ Alarm clock or ○ My parents wake me up?

Remarkable Room!

What does your space say about you?

1. Do you ⊚ Share a room or ◯ Have your own space?

2. Who chose the décor? ◯ Me ◯ My sibling or ⊛ My parents

3. The color scheme in my room is _Blue and Pink_

4. Is your room ◯ Really girly and pink or ⊙ Not feminine at all?

5. If you hung an animal poster on your wall, would it be a

   ◯ Puppy or ◯ Kitten?

6. Do you like posters of ◯ Celebrities

   ◯ Animals or ◯ Bands?

7. ◯ Painted walls or ◯ Wallpaper?

8. ◯ Glow-in-the-dark sticker stars or

   ◯ Blue sky and fluffy white clouds?

9. Are your siblings allowed in your room? ◯ Sure ◯ Only

   if they knock first or ◯ Absolutely not!

10. Is your room ◯ Neat and organized ◯ A total pigsty or

    ◯ It depends on my mood?

11. Do you clean your room ◯ Once a week ◯ Once a month or

    ◯ Only when my parents make me?

12. ◯ A TV in your room or ◯ No such luck?

13. Do you ◯ Have your own computer or ◯ Have to share?

14. When you call your friends, do you use ◯ Your cell phone

    ◯ Your bedroom phone or ◯ The house phone?

15. Do you write in a ◯ Journal ◯ Diary or ◯ Blog?

16. What's more important to you: ○ Phone ○ TV or
    ○ Computer?

17. ○ Your favorite TV show or ○ A great movie?

18. Do your homework ○ At your desk ○ On your bed or
    ○ Somewhere else in the house?

19. ○ Your own bathroom or ○ I wish!?

20. ○ Top bunk or ○ Bottom bunk?

21. ○ Twin-size bed or ○ Full-size bed?

22. ○ Lots of pillows or ○ Only one?

23. Before bed, do you ○ Read ○ Listen to music or
    ○ Watch TV?

24. Are you ○ An early bird or ○ A night owl?

25. When you sleep, do you ○ Leave the door open
    ○ Open it a crack or ○ It's got to be closed?

26. Do you sleep on your ○ Stomach ○ Side or ○ Back?

27. Do you snore? ○ Yes ○ No or ○ How would I know?

28. Do you sleep with a stuffed animal or special blanket?
    ○ No way! ○ Yes, and it's no big deal or ○ I'll never admit it
    even if I do!

29. Do you use a night-light? ○ Are you kidding? ○ Um yeah,
    but don't tell!

30. ○ Alarm clock or ○ My parents wake me up?

Remarkable Room!
What does your space say about you?

1. Do you ◯ Share a room or ◉ Have your own space?

2. Who chose the décor? ◯ Me ◉ My sibling or ◯ My parents

3. The color scheme in my room is _____.

4. Is your room ◯ Really girly and pink or ◯ Not feminine at all?

5. If you hung an animal poster on your wall, would it be a
   ◯ Puppy or ◯ Kitten?

6. Do you like posters of ◯ Celebrities
   ◯ Animals or ◯ Bands?

7. ◯ Painted walls or ◯ Wallpaper?

8. ◯ Glow-in-the-dark sticker stars or
   ◯ Blue sky and fluffy white clouds?

9. Are your siblings allowed in your room? ◯ Sure ◯ Only
   if they knock first or ◯ Absolutely not!

10. Is your room ◯ Neat and organized ◯ A total pigsty or
    ◯ It depends on my mood?

11. Do you clean your room ◯ Once a week ◯ Once a month or
    ◯ Only when my parents make me?

12. ◯ A TV in your room or ◯ No such luck?

13. Do you ◯ Have your own computer or ◯ Have to share?

14. When you call your friends, do you use ◯ Your cell phone
    ◯ Your bedroom phone or ◯ The house phone?

15. Do you write in a ◯ Journal ◯ Diary or ◯ Blog?

16. What's more important to you: ⚪ Phone ⚪ TV or ⚪ Computer?

17. ⚪ Your favorite TV show or ⚪ A great movie?

18. Do your homework ⚪ At your desk ⚪ On your bed or ⚪ Somewhere else in the house?

19. ⚪ Your own bathroom or ⚪ I wish!?

20. ⚪ Top bunk or ⚪ Bottom bunk?

21. ⚪ Twin-size bed or ⚪ Full-size bed?

22. ⚪ Lots of pillows or ⚪ Only one?

23. Before bed, do you ⚪ Read ⚪ Listen to music or ⚪ Watch TV?

24. Are you ⚪ An early bird or ⚪ A night owl?

25. When you sleep, do you ⚪ Leave the door open ⚪ Open it a crack or ⚪ It's got to be closed?

26. Do you sleep on your ⚪ Stomach ⚪ Side or ⚪ Back?

27. Do you snore? ⚪ Yes ⚪ No or ⚪ How would I know?

28. Do you sleep with a stuffed animal or special blanket? ⚪ No way! ⚪ Yes, and it's no big deal or ⚪ I'll never admit it even if I do!

29. Do you use a night-light? ⚪ Are you kidding? ⚪ Um yeah, but don't tell!

30. ⚪ Alarm clock or ⚪ My parents wake me up?

Fright Fest!
Are you a scaredy cat?

1. Are you more scared of ⊙ Vampires or ◯ Werewolves?

2. ⊙ Zombies or ◯ Ghosts?

3. ⊙ The dark or ◯ Heights?

4. ◯ Small spaces or ⊙ Big crowds?

5. ◯ Dogs or ⊙ Visiting the doctor?

6. ⊙ Speaking in public or ◯ Being alone?

7. ◯ Flying on an airplane or ⊙ A bad thunderstorm?

8. ◯ Sharks or ⊙ Jellyfish?

9. ⊙ Spiders or ◯ Snakes?

10. ◯ Mice or ⊙ Bats?

11. Would you rather grow ⊙ Fangs or ◯ Hair everywhere?

12. Would you rather eat a ◯ Beetle or ⊙ Worm?

13. ⊙ Dog food or ◯ Brussels sprouts?

14. Would you rather walk alone through a ◯ Haunted house or ⊙ Deserted graveyard?

15. How do you feel about roller coasters? ⊙ OMG, I love them! or ◯ They're the worst.

16. ◉ Ferris wheel or ◯ Merry-go-round?

17. Are you superstitious? ◉ No way or ◯ Yes! Don't tell!

18. Would you rather ◯ Walk under a ladder or
    ◉ Have a black cat cross your path?

19. If you see a penny on the sidewalk, do you pick it up?
    ◉ If it's heads up or ◯ Yes! You may need one later.

20. What's worse: ◯ Opening an umbrella indoors or
    ◉ Breaking a mirror?

Friday the 13th

21. What do you think of Friday the 13th? ◉ It's an unlucky
    day or ◯ It's just like any other Friday!

22. Scary movies ◯ Rock! or ◉ Give me nightmares?

23. When you're nervous, do you ◯ Bite your nails or
    ◉ Pace back and forth?

24. What's scarier: ◉ A pop quiz or ◉ A final exam?

25. ◯ The first day at a new school or ◉ Singing a solo in
    the school concert?

26. ◯ Yelled at by a teacher or ◉ Called to the principal's office

27. ◉ A failing grade or ◯ Being caught cheating?

28. ◯ Grounded for a month or ◉ No TV and computer for a we

29. Which nightmare is worse: ◯ Falling from a building or
    ◉ Having all your teeth fall out?

30. What's the scariest thing you've ever done?

when I rode the raging bull

Fright Fest!

Are you a scaredy cat?

1. Are you more scared of ⬤ Vampires or ⬤ Werewolves?

2. ⬤ Zombies or ⬤ Ghosts?

3. ⬤ The dark or ⬤ Heights?

4. ⬤ Small spaces or ⬤ Big crowds?

5. ⬤ Dogs or ⬤ Visiting the doctor?

6. ⬤ Speaking in public or ⬤ Being alone?

7. ⬤ Flying on an airplane or ⬤ A bad thunderstorm?

8. ⬤ Sharks or ⬤ Jellyfish?

9. ⬤ Spiders or ⬤ Snakes?

10. ⬤ Mice or ⬤ Bats?

11. Would you rather grow ⬤ Fangs or ⬤ Hair everywhere?

12. Would you rather eat a ⬤ Beetle or ⬤ Worm?

13. ⬤ Dog food or ⬤ Brussels sprouts?

14. Would you rather walk alone through a ⬤ Haunted house or ⬤ Deserted graveyard?

15. How do you feel about roller coasters? ⬤ OMG, I love

16. ◯ Ferris wheel or ◯ Merry-go-round?

17. Are you superstitious? ◯ No way or ◯ Yes! Don't tell!

18. Would you rather ◯ Walk under a ladder or
    ◯ Have a black cat cross your path?

19. If you see a penny on the sidewalk, do you pick it up?
    ◯ If it's heads up or ◯ Yes! You may need one later.

20. What's worse: ◯ Opening an umbrella indoors or
    ◯ Breaking a mirror?

Friday the 13th

21. What do you think of Friday the 13th? ◯ It's an unlucky
    day or ◯ It's just like any other Friday!

22. Scary movies ◯ Rock! or ◯ Give me nightmares?

23. When you're nervous, do you ◯ Bite your nails or
    ◯ Pace back and forth?

24. What's scarier: ◯ A pop quiz or ◯ A final exam?

25. ◯ The first day at a new school or ◯ Singing a solo in
    the school concert?

26. ◯ Yelled at by a teacher or ◯ Called to the principal's office

27. ◯ A failing grade or ◯ Being caught cheating?

28. ◯ Grounded for a month or ◯ No TV and computer for a we

29. Which nightmare is worse: ◯ Falling from a building or
    ◯ Having all your teeth fall out?

30. What's the scariest thing you've ever done?

_____

Fright Fest!

Are you a scaredy cat?

1. Are you more scared of ⬤ Vampires or ⬤ Werewolves?

2. ⬤ Zombies or ⬤ Ghosts?

3. ⬤ The dark or ⬤ Heights?

4. ⬤ Small spaces or ⬤ Big crowds?

5. ⬤ Dogs or ⬤ Visiting the doctor?

6. ⬤ Speaking in public or ⬤ Being alone?

7. ⬤ Flying on an airplane or ⬤ A bad thunderstorm?

8. ⬤ Sharks or ⬤ Jellyfish?

9. ⬤ Spiders or ⬤ Snakes?

10. ⬤ Mice or ⬤ Bats?

11. Would you rather grow ⬤ Fangs or ⬤ Hair everywhere?

12. Would you rather eat a ⬤ Beetle or ⬤ Worm?

13. ⬤ Dog food or ⬤ Brussels sprouts?

14. Would you rather walk alone through a ⬤ Haunted house or ⬤ Deserted graveyard?

15. How do you feel about roller coasters? ⬤ OMG, I love them! or ⬤ They're the worst.

16. ⚪ Ferris wheel or ⚪ Merry-go-round?

17. Are you superstitious? ⚪ No way or ⚪ Yes! Don't tell!

18. Would you rather ⚪ Walk under a ladder or

    ⚪ Have a black cat cross your path?

19. If you see a penny on the sidewalk, do you pick it up?

    ⚪ If it's heads up or ⚪ Yes! You may need one later.

20. What's worse: ⚪ Opening an umbrella indoors or

    ⚪ Breaking a mirror?

    Friday the 13th

21. What do you think of Friday the 13th? ⚪ It's an unlucky

    day or ⚪ It's just like any other Friday!

22. Scary movies ⚪ Rock! or ⚪ Give me nightmares?

23. When you're nervous, do you ⚪ Bite your nails or

    ⚪ Pace back and forth?

24. What's scarier: ⚪ A pop quiz or ⚪ A final exam?

25. ⚪ The first day at a new school or ⚪ Singing a solo in

    the school concert?

26. ⚪ Yelled at by a teacher or ⚪ Called to the principal's office

27. ⚪ A failing grade or ⚪ Being caught cheating?

28. ⚪ Grounded for a month or ⚪ No TV and computer for a we

29. Which nightmare is worse: ⚪ Falling from a building or

    ⚪ Having all your teeth fall out?

30. What's the scariest thing you've ever done?

    _____

Fright Fest!
Are you a scaredy cat?

1. Are you more scared of ⚪ Vampires or ⚪ Werewolves?

2. ⚪ Zombies or ⚪ Ghosts?

3. ⚪ The dark or ⚪ Heights?

4. ⚪ Small spaces or ⚪ Big crowds?

5. ⚪ Dogs or ⚪ Visiting the doctor?

6. ⚪ Speaking in public or ⚪ Being alone?

7. ⚪ Flying on an airplane or ⚪ A bad thunderstorm?

8. ⚪ Sharks or ⚪ Jellyfish?

9. ⚪ Spiders or ⚪ Snakes?

10. ⚪ Mice or ⚪ Bats?

11. Would you rather grow ⚪ Fangs or ⚪ Hair everywhere?

12. Would you rather eat a ⚪ Beetle or ⚪ Worm?

13. ⚪ Dog food or ⚪ Brussels sprouts?

14. Would you rather walk alone through a ⚪ Haunted house or ⚪ Deserted graveyard?

15. How do you feel about roller coasters? ⚪ OMG, I love them! or ⚪ They're the worst.

16. ⚪ Ferris wheel or ⚪ Merry-go-round?

17. Are you superstitious? ⚪ No way or ⚪ Yes! Don't tell!

18. Would you rather ⚪ Walk under a ladder or

⚪ Have a black cat cross your path?

19. If you see a penny on the sidewalk, do you pick it up?

⚪ If it's heads up or ⚪ Yes! You may need one later.

20. What's worse: ⚪ Opening an umbrella indoors or

⚪ Breaking a mirror?

Friday the 13th

21. What do you think of Friday the 13th? ⚪ It's an unlucky

day or ⚪ It's just like any other Friday!

22. Scary movies ⚪ Rock! or ⚪ Give me nightmares?

23. When you're nervous, do you ⚪ Bite your nails or

⚪ Pace back and forth?

24. What's scarier: ⚪ A pop quiz or ⚪ A final exam?

25. ⚪ The first day at a new school or ⚪ Singing a solo in

the school concert?

26. ⚪ Yelled at by a teacher or ⚪ Called to the principal's office

27. ⚪ A failing grade or ⚪ Being caught cheating?

28. ⚪ Grounded for a month or ⚪ No TV and computer for a w

29. Which nightmare is worse: ⚪ Falling from a building or

⚪ Having all your teeth fall out?

30. What's the scariest thing you've ever done?

_____

Sleepover Secrets
Shhh! Don't tell!

1. Would you rather have a sleepover with ○ Just one friend or ● The more, the merrier?

2. What's the best thing about sleepovers: ○ Giggling about boys ○ Eating junk food or ● Staying up late?

3. Have you ever prank called a boy? ○ Totally! ○ I'm not that brave or ○ I plead the fifth.

4. ● Truth or ○ Dare?

5. What's the best "truth" question? _____
   _____

6. What's your favorite dare? _____
   _____

7. ○ MASH or ○ Charades?

8. ● Video games or ○ Board games?

9. ● Karaoke or ○ Dance contest?

10. ○ Pillow fight or ● Jump on the beds?

11. Midnight ○ Makeovers or ● Movies?

12. ● Ghost stories or ○ Boy talk?

13. ○ Tell the ghost story or ● Listen to someone else?

14. When you want a snack, do you go for ○ Pizza or ● Ice cream?

15. Fave pizza topping: ● Cheese ○ Pepperoni or ○ Veggie?

16. If you're making sundaes, do you start with
⬤ Chocolate ◯ Vanilla or ◯ Strawberry ice cream?

17. ◯ Peanut butter or ⬤ Chocolate fudge?

18. ⬤ Whipped cream or ◯ A cherry on top?

19. ⬤ Popcorn or ◯ Chips and dip?

20. Are you usually ⬤ The last to fall asleep or
◯ The first to drift off?

21. Do you ⬤ Stay up all night or ◯ Sleep a little bit?

22. ◯ Indoor sleepover or ⬤ Backyard tent campout?

23. ⬤ Sleeping bag or ◯ I'll take the bed, please?

24. ⬤ Pajamas or ◯ T-shirt and sweatpants?

25. ⬤ Bunny slippers or ◯ Socks?

26. Do you wake up ⬤ First or ◯ Last?

27. For breakfast, do you prefer ⬤ Pancakes or
◯ Waffles?

28. ◯ Eggs sunny-side up or ⬤ Scrambled?

29. ◯ Hot oatmeal or ⬤ Cold cornflakes?

30. Do you take a nap the next day? ◯ Definitely! or
⬤ R U kidding? I'm not in kindergarten!

Sleepover Secrets
Shhh! Don't tell!

1. Would you rather have a sleepover with ◯ Just one friend or ◯ The more, the merrier?

2. What's the best thing about sleepovers: ◯ Giggling about boys ◯ Eating junk food or ◯ Staying up late?

3. Have you ever prank called a boy? ◯ Totally! ◯ I'm not that brave or ◯ I plead the fifth.

4. ◯ Truth or ◯ Dare?

5. What's the best "truth" question?_____ _____

6. What's your favorite dare?_____ _____

7. ◯ MASH or ◯ Charades?

8. ◯ Video games or ◯ Board games?

9. ◯ Karaoke or ◯ Dance contest?

10. ◯ Pillow fight or ◯ Jump on the beds?

11. Midnight ◯ Makeovers or ◯ Movies?

12. ◯ Ghost stories or ◯ Boy talk?

13. ◯ Tell the ghost story or ◯ Listen to someone else?

14. When you want a snack, do you go for ◯ Pizza or ◯ Ice cream?

15. Fave pizza topping: ◯ Cheese ◯ Pepperoni or ◯ Veggie?

16. If you're making sundaes, do you start with
    ○ Chocolate ○ Vanilla or ○ Strawberry ice cream?
17. ○ Peanut butter or ○ Chocolate fudge?
18. ○ Whipped cream or ○ A cherry on top?
19. ○ Popcorn or ○ Chips and dip?
20. Are you usually ○ The last to fall asleep or
    ○ The first to drift off?
21. Do you ○ Stay up all night or ○ Sleep a little bit?
22. ○ Indoor sleepover or ○ Backyard tent campout?
23. ○ Sleeping bag or ○ I'll take the bed, please?
24. ○ Pajamas or ○ T-shirt and sweatpants?
25. ○ Bunny slippers or ○ Socks?
26. Do you wake up ○ First or ○ Last?
27. For breakfast, do you prefer ○ Pancakes or
    ○ Waffles?
28. ○ Eggs sunny-side up or ○ Scrambled?
29. ○ Hot oatmeal or ○ Cold cornflakes?
30. Do you take a nap the next day? ○ Definitely! or
    ○ R U kidding? I'm not in kindergarten!

Sleepover Secrets
Shhh! Don't tell!

1. Would you rather have a sleepover with ◯ Just one friend or ◯ The more, the merrier?

2. What's the best thing about sleepovers: ◯ Giggling about boys ◯ Eating junk food or ◯ Staying up late?

3. Have you ever prank called a boy? ◯ Totally! ◯ I'm not that brave or ◯ I plead the fifth.

4. ◯ Truth or ◯ Dare?

5. What's the best "truth" question?_____
_____

6. What's your favorite dare?_____
_____

7. ◯ MASH or ◯ Charades?

8. ◯ Video games or ◯ Board games?

9. ◯ Karaoke or ◯ Dance contest?

10. ◯ Pillow fight or ◯ Jump on the beds?

11. Midnight ◯ Makeovers or ◯ Movies?

12. ◯ Ghost stories or ◯ Boy talk?

13. ◯ Tell the ghost story or ◯ Listen to someone else?

14. When you want a snack, do you go for ◯ Pizza or ◯ Ice cream?

15. Fave pizza topping: ◯ Cheese ◯ Pepperoni or ◯ Veggie?

16. If you're making sundaes, do you start with ○ Chocolate ○ Vanilla or ○ Strawberry ice cream?

17. ○ Peanut butter or ○ Chocolate fudge?

18. ○ Whipped cream or ○ A cherry on top?

19. ○ Popcorn or ○ Chips and dip?

20. Are you usually ○ The last to fall asleep or ○ The first to drift off?

21. Do you ○ Stay up all night or ○ Sleep a little bit?

22. ○ Indoor sleepover or ○ Backyard tent campout?

23. ○ Sleeping bag or ○ I'll take the bed, please?

24. ○ Pajamas or ○ T-shirt and sweatpants?

25. ○ Bunny slippers or ○ Socks?

26. Do you wake up ○ First or ○ Last?

27. For breakfast, do you prefer ○ Pancakes or ○ Waffles?

28. ○ Eggs sunny-side up or ○ Scrambled?

29. ○ Hot oatmeal or ○ Cold cornflakes?

30. Do you take a nap the next day? ○ Definitely! or ○ R U kidding? I'm not in kindergarten!

Sleepover Secrets
Shhh! Don't tell!

1. Would you rather have a sleepover with ○ Just one friend or ○ The more, the merrier?

2. What's the best thing about sleepovers: ○ Giggling about boys ○ Eating junk food or ○ Staying up late?

3. Have you ever prank called a boy? ○ Totally! ○ I'm not that brave or ○ I plead the fifth.

4. ○ Truth or ○ Dare?

5. What's the best "truth" question?_____ _____

6. What's your favorite dare?_____ _____

7. ○ MASH or ○ Charades?

8. ○ Video games or ○ Board games?

9. ○ Karaoke or ○ Dance contest?

10. ○ Pillow fight or ○ Jump on the beds?

11. Midnight ○ Makeovers or ○ Movies?

12. ○ Ghost stories or ○ Boy talk?

13. ○ Tell the ghost story or ○ Listen to someone else?

14. When you want a snack, do you go for ○ Pizza or ○ Ice cream?

15. Fave pizza topping: ○ Cheese ○ Pepperoni or ○ Veggie?

16. If you're making sundaes, do you start with
    ○ Chocolate ○ Vanilla or ○ Strawberry ice cream?
17. ○ Peanut butter or ○ Chocolate fudge?
18. ○ Whipped cream or ○ A cherry on top?
19. ○ Popcorn or ○ Chips and dip?
20. Are you usually ○ The last to fall asleep or
    ○ The first to drift off?
21. Do you ○ Stay up all night or ○ Sleep a little bit?
22. ○ Indoor sleepover or ○ Backyard tent campout?
23. ○ Sleeping bag or ○ I'll take the bed, please?
24. ○ Pajamas or ○ T-shirt and sweatpants?
25. ○ Bunny slippers or ○ Socks?
26. Do you wake up ○ First or ○ Last?
27. For breakfast, do you prefer ○ Pancakes or
    ○ Waffles?
28. ○ Eggs sunny-side up or ○ Scrambled?
29. ○ Hot oatmeal or ○ Cold cornflakes?
30. Do you take a nap the next day? ○ Definitely! or
    ○ R U kidding? I'm not in kindergarten!

Who's Got Talent?
You do, that's who!

1. Would you rather watch ⚪ *American Idol* ⚪ *So You Think You Can Dance* or ⚪ *Dancing with the Stars*?

2. If you were a reality show judge, would you be ⚪ Kind and encouraging or ⚪ Brutally honest?

3. Would you rather be able to ⚪ Sing or ⚪ Dance?

4. ⚪ Play an instrument or ⚪ Act?

5. ⚪ Juggle ⚪ Ride a unicycle or ⚪ Do both?

6. ⚪ Twirl a baton or ⚪ Walk on stilts?

7. ⚪ Tell great jokes or ⚪ Do magic tricks?

8. ⚪ Shoot a three-pointer or ⚪ Run a six-minute mile?

9. ⚪ Speak five different languages or ⚪ Understand ten?

10. When you sing along to your favorite song in your bedroom, do you ⚪ Lip-synch or ⚪ Belt it out?

11. Do you get stage fright? ⚪ No, I love the spotlight or ⚪ Yes, performing in front of other people is terrifying!

12. When you see your parents in the audience, do you ⚪ Wave and smile or ⚪ Wince and try to hide?

13. How do you deal with your stage fright? ⚪ Pretend everyone is in their underwear or ⚪ Focus on the back row.

14. At your school, do teachers perform in your talent shows? ⚪ Yes, and it's really fun or ⚪ No, but I wish they did!

15. Which teacher would you love to see onstage? _____

16. Would you rather ○ Help build the set for the school play or ○ Design the costumes?

17. ○ Musical or ○ Drama?

18. ● Romance or ◐ Comedy?

19. ○ Sing in the school musical or ○ Play an instrument in the orchestra?

20. Play the role of ◐ An old person or ● A male character?

21. ◐ Villain or ● Hero?

22. What would you think if you had to perform a scene onstage with your crush? ◐ OMG, I'd love it! or ● I would die of embarrassment!

23. What would be worse: ◐ Losing your voice on opening night or ● Forgetting all your lines?

24. ● Your pants splitting open onstage or ◐ Accidentally spitting on one of the other cast members?

25. ◐ Hitting the wrong note in your solo or ● Burping loudly while onstage?

26. If you and your friends formed a band, would you rather ◐ Be the lead singer or ● Sing backup?

27. Would you rather write the ● Lyrics or ◐ Music?

28. Would you rather play ◐ Lead guitar or ● Bass guitar?

29. ● Drums or ◐ Keyboard?

30. What would your band's name be? _The rock stars_

Who's Got Talent?
You do, that's who!

1. Would you rather watch ◯ *American Idol* ◯ *So You Think You Can Dance* or ◯ *Dancing with the Stars*?

2. If you were a reality show judge, would you be ◯ Kind and encouraging or ◯ Brutally honest?

3. Would you rather be able to ◯ Sing or ◯ Dance?

4. ◯ Play an instrument or ◯ Act?

5. ◯ Juggle ◯ Ride a unicycle or ◯ Do both?

6. ◯ Twirl a baton or ◯ Walk on stilts?

7. ◯ Tell great jokes or ◯ Do magic tricks?

8. ◯ Shoot a three-pointer or ◯ Run a six-minute mile?

9. ◯ Speak five different languages or ◯ Understand ten?

10. When you sing along to your favorite song in your bedroom, do you ◯ Lip-synch or ◯ Belt it out?

11. Do you get stage fright? ◯ No, I love the spotlight or ◯ Yes, performing in front of other people is terrifying!

12. When you see your parents in the audience, do you ◯ Wave and smile or ◯ Wince and try to hide?

13. How do you deal with your stage fright? ◯ Pretend everyone is in their underwear or ◯ Focus on the back row.

14. At your school, do teachers perform in your talent shows? ◯ Yes, and it's really fun or ◯ No, but I wish they did!

15. Which teacher would you love to see onstage? _____

16. Would you rather ⬤ Help build the set for the school play or ⬤ Design the costumes?

17. ⬤ Musical or ⬤ Drama?

18. ⬤ Romance or ⬤ Comedy?

19. ⬤ Sing in the school musical or ⬤ Play an instrument in the orchestra?

20. Play the role of ⬤ An old person or ⬤ A male character?

21. ⬤ Villain or ⬤ Hero?

22. What would you think if you had to perform a scene onstage with your crush? ⬤ OMG, I'd love it! or ⬤ I would die of embarrassment!

23. What would be worse: ⬤ Losing your voice on opening night or ⬤ Forgetting all your lines?

24. ⬤ Your pants splitting open onstage or ⬤ Accidentally spitting on one of the other cast members?

25. ⬤ Hitting the wrong note in your solo or ⬤ Burping loudly while onstage?

26. If you and your friends formed a band, would you rather ⬤ Be the lead singer or ⬤ Sing backup?

27. Would you rather write the ⬤ Lyrics or ⬤ Music?

28. Would you rather play ⬤ Lead guitar or ⬤ Bass guitar?

29. ⬤ Drums or ⬤ Keyboard?

30. What would your band's name be? _____

Who's Got Talent?
You do, that's who!

1. Would you rather watch ⬤ *American Idol* ⬤ *So You Think You Can Dance* or ⬤ *Dancing with the Stars?*

2. If you were a reality show judge, would you be ⬤ Kind and encouraging or ⬤ Brutally honest?

3. Would you rather be able to ⬤ Sing or ⬤ Dance?

4. ⬤ Play an instrument or ⬤ Act?

5. ⬤ Juggle ⬤ Ride a unicycle or ⬤ Do both?

6. ⬤ Twirl a baton or ⬤ Walk on stilts?

7. ⬤ Tell great jokes or ⬤ Do magic tricks?

8. ⬤ Shoot a three-pointer or ⬤ Run a six-minute mile?

9. ⬤ Speak five different languages or ⬤ Understand ten?

10. When you sing along to your favorite song in your bedroom, do you ⬤ Lip-synch or ⬤ Belt it out?

11. Do you get stage fright? ⬤ No, I love the spotlight or ⬤ Yes, performing in front of other people is terrifying!

12. When you see your parents in the audience, do you ⬤ Wave and smile or ⬤ Wince and try to hide?

13. How do you deal with your stage fright? ⬤ Pretend everyone is in their underwear or ⬤ Focus on the back row.

14. At your school, do teachers perform in your talent shows? ⬤ Yes, and it's really fun or ⬤ No, but I wish they did!

15. Which teacher would you love to see onstage? _____

16. Would you rather ⬤ Help build the set for the school play or ⬤ Design the costumes?

17. ⬤ Musical or ⬤ Drama?

18. ⬤ Romance or ⬤ Comedy?

19. ⬤ Sing in the school musical or ⬤ Play an instrument in the orchestra?

20. Play the role of ⬤ An old person or ⬤ A male character?

21. ⬤ Villain or ⬤ Hero?

22. What would you think if you had to perform a scene onstage with your crush? ⬤ OMG, I'd love it! or ⬤ I would die of embarrassment!

23. What would be worse: ⬤ Losing your voice on opening night or ⬤ Forgetting all your lines?

24. ⬤ Your pants splitting open onstage or ⬤ Accidentally spitting on one of the other cast members?

25. ⬤ Hitting the wrong note in your solo or ⬤ Burping loudly while onstage?

26. If you and your friends formed a band, would you rather ⬤ Be the lead singer or ⬤ Sing backup?

27. Would you rather write the ⬤ Lyrics or ⬤ Music?

28. Would you rather play ⬤ Lead guitar or ⬤ Bass guitar?

29. ⬤ Drums or ⬤ Keyboard?

30. What would your band's name be? _____

Who's Got Talent?
You do, that's who!

1. Would you rather watch ○ *American Idol* ○ *So You Think You Can Dance* or ○ *Dancing with the Stars?*

2. If you were a reality show judge, would you be ○ Kind and encouraging or ○ Brutally honest?

3. Would you rather be able to ○ Sing or ○ Dance?

4. ○ Play an instrument or ○ Act?

5. ○ Juggle ○ Ride a unicycle or ○ Do both?

6. ○ Twirl a baton or ○ Walk on stilts?

7. ○ Tell great jokes or ○ Do magic tricks?

8. ○ Shoot a three-pointer or ○ Run a six-minute mile?

9. ○ Speak five different languages or ○ Understand ten?

10. When you sing along to your favorite song in your bedroom, do you ○ Lip-synch or ○ Belt it out?

11. Do you get stage fright? ○ No, I love the spotlight or ○ Yes, performing in front of other people is terrifying!

12. When you see your parents in the audience, do you ○ Wave and smile or ○ Wince and try to hide?

13. How do you deal with your stage fright? ○ Pretend everyone is in their underwear or ○ Focus on the back row.

14. At your school, do teachers perform in your talent shows? ○ Yes, and it's really fun or ○ No, but I wish they did!

15. Which teacher would you love to see onstage? _____

16. Would you rather ⬤ Help build the set for the school play or ⬤ Design the costumes?

17. ⬤ Musical or ⬤ Drama?

18. ⬤ Romance or ⬤ Comedy?

19. ⬤ Sing in the school musical or ⬤ Play an instrument in the orchestra?

20. Play the role of ⬤ An old person or ⬤ A male character?

21. ⬤ Villain or ⬤ Hero?

22. What would you think if you had to perform a scene onstage with your crush? ⬤ OMG, I'd love it! or ⬤ I would die of embarrassment!

23. What would be worse: ⬤ Losing your voice on opening night or ⬤ Forgetting all your lines?

24. ⬤ Your pants splitting open onstage or ⬤ Accidentally spitting on one of the other cast members?

25. ⬤ Hitting the wrong note in your solo or ⬤ Burping loudly while onstage?

26. If you and your friends formed a band, would you rather ⬤ Be the lead singer or ⬤ Sing backup?

27. Would you rather write the ⬤ Lyrics or ⬤ Music?

28. Would you rather play ⬤ Lead guitar or ⬤ Bass guitar?

29. ⬤ Drums or ⬤ Keyboard?

30. What would your band's name be? _____

After the Bell
What do you do after school?

1. After school, are you most likely to be found
   - ● Doing something creative or ○ On the athletic fields?

2. ○ Student Government or ● Art Club?

3. ● Astronomy Club or ○ Chess Club?

4. ● Cheerleading or ○ Spanish Club?

5. ○ Math Team or ● Robotics Club?

6. ● Theater or ○ Band?

7. ● Soccer or ○ Softball?

8. ● Basketball or ○ Volleyball?

9. ● Swimming or ○ Track?

10. Write for the ○ Newspaper or ● Yearbook?

11. When your favorite club holds elections for officer

    positions, are you ○ The first one to raise your hand or

    ● The one hiding in the back of the room?

12. When you first get home from school, do you

    ● Grab a snack or ○ Check your e-mail?

13. ○ Do your homework right away ○ Watch TV

    or ● Hang out with friends first?

14. Who is the first person in the family to get home?

    ● It's usually me or ○ My parents are already there.

15. ○ Do your chores right away or ● Put them off

    until the last possible minute?

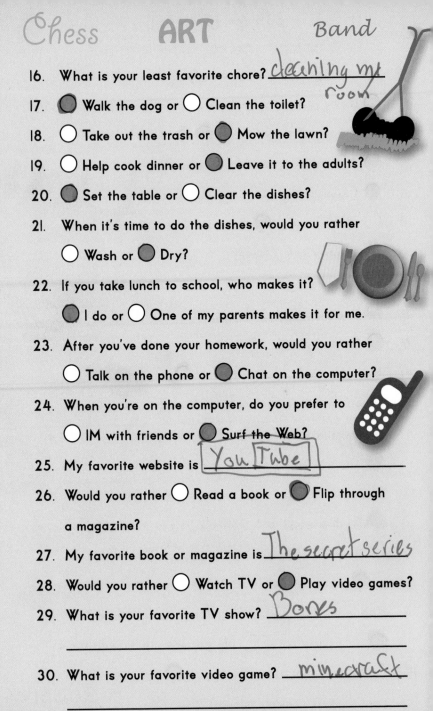

Chess   ART   Band

16. What is your least favorite chore? _cleaning my room_

17. ◉ Walk the dog or ○ Clean the toilet?

18. ○ Take out the trash or ◉ Mow the lawn?

19. ○ Help cook dinner or ◉ Leave it to the adults?

20. ◉ Set the table or ○ Clear the dishes?

21. When it's time to do the dishes, would you rather
     ○ Wash or ◉ Dry?

22. If you take lunch to school, who makes it?
     ◉ I do or ○ One of my parents makes it for me.

23. After you've done your homework, would you rather
     ○ Talk on the phone or ◉ Chat on the computer?

24. When you're on the computer, do you prefer to
     ○ IM with friends or ◉ Surf the Web?

25. My favorite website is _You Tube_

26. Would you rather ○ Read a book or ◉ Flip through
     a magazine?

27. My favorite book or magazine is _The secret series_

28. Would you rather ○ Watch TV or ◉ Play video games?

29. What is your favorite TV show? _Bones_
     _____

30. What is your favorite video game? _minecraft_
     _____

After the Bell
What do you do after school?

1. After school, are you most likely to be found

    ○ Doing something creative or ○ On the athletic fields?

2. ○ Student Government or ○ Art Club?

3. ○ Astronomy Club or ○ Chess Club?

4. ○ Cheerleading or ○ Spanish Club?

5. ○ Math Team or ○ Robotics Club?

6. ○ Theater or ○ Band?

7. ○ Soccer or ○ Softball?

8. ○ Basketball or ○ Volleyball?

9. ○ Swimming or ○ Track?

10. Write for the ○ Newspaper or ○ Yearbook?

11. When your favorite club holds elections for officer

    positions, are you ○ The first one to raise your hand or

    ○ The one hiding in the back of the room?

12. When you first get home from school, do you

    ○ Grab a snack or ○ Check your e-mail?

13. ○ Do your homework right away ○ Watch TV

    or ○ Hang out with friends first?

14. Who is the first person in the family to get home?

    ○ It's usually me or ○ My parents are already there.

15. ○ Do your chores right away or ○ Put them off

    until the last possible minute?

Swim

Math

Robotics

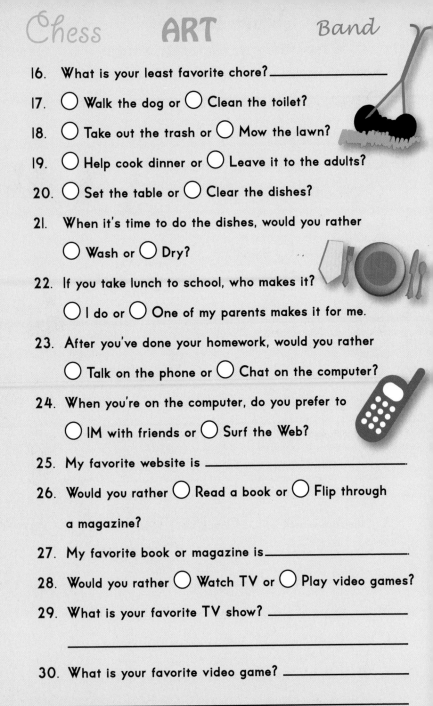

16. What is your least favorite chore?_____

17. ◯ Walk the dog or ◯ Clean the toilet?

18. ◯ Take out the trash or ◯ Mow the lawn?

19. ◯ Help cook dinner or ◯ Leave it to the adults?

20. ◯ Set the table or ◯ Clear the dishes?

21. When it's time to do the dishes, would you rather

    ◯ Wash or ◯ Dry?

22. If you take lunch to school, who makes it?

    ◯ I do or ◯ One of my parents makes it for me.

23. After you've done your homework, would you rather

    ◯ Talk on the phone or ◯ Chat on the computer?

24. When you're on the computer, do you prefer to

    ◯ IM with friends or ◯ Surf the Web?

25. My favorite website is _____.

26. Would you rather ◯ Read a book or ◯ Flip through

    a magazine?

27. My favorite book or magazine is_____.

28. Would you rather ◯ Watch TV or ◯ Play video games?

29. What is your favorite TV show? _____

    _____

30. What is your favorite video game? _____

    _____

After the Bell
What do you do after school?

1. After school, are you most likely to be found
   - ○ Doing something creative or ○ On the athletic fields?

2. ○ Student Government or ○ Art Club?

3. ○ Astronomy Club or ○ Chess Club?

4. ○ Cheerleading or ○ Spanish Club?

5. ○ Math Team or ○ Robotics Club?

6. ○ Theater or ○ Band?

7. ○ Soccer or ○ Softball?

8. ○ Basketball or ○ Volleyball?

9. ○ Swimming or ○ Track?

10. Write for the ○ Newspaper or ○ Yearbook?

11. When your favorite club holds elections for officer positions, are you ○ The first one to raise your hand or ○ The one hiding in the back of the room?

12. When you first get home from school, do you ○ Grab a snack or ○ Check your e-mail?

13. ○ Do your homework right away ○ Watch TV or ○ Hang out with friends first?

14. Who is the first person in the family to get home? ○ It's usually me or ○ My parents are already there.

15. ○ Do your chores right away or ○ Put them off until the last possible minute?

Swim

Math

Robotics

Chess ART Band

16. What is your least favorite chore? _____

17. ◯ Walk the dog or ◯ Clean the toilet?

18. ◯ Take out the trash or ◯ Mow the lawn?

19. ◯ Help cook dinner or ◯ Leave it to the adults?

20. ◯ Set the table or ◯ Clear the dishes?

21. When it's time to do the dishes, would you rather

◯ Wash or ◯ Dry?

22. If you take lunch to school, who makes it?

◯ I do or ◯ One of my parents makes it for me.

23. After you've done your homework, would you rather

◯ Talk on the phone or ◯ Chat on the computer?

24. When you're on the computer, do you prefer to

◯ IM with friends or ◯ Surf the Web?

25. My favorite website is _____

26. Would you rather ◯ Read a book or ◯ Flip through

a magazine?

27. My favorite book or magazine is _____

28. Would you rather ◯ Watch TV or ◯ Play video games?

29. What is your favorite TV show? _____

_____

30. What is your favorite video game? _____

_____

After the Bell
What do you do after school?

1. After school, are you most likely to be found

    ○ Doing something creative or ○ On the athletic fields?

2. ○ Student Government or ○ Art Club?

3. ○ Astronomy Club or ○ Chess Club?

4. ○ Cheerleading or ○ Spanish Club?

5. ○ Math Team or ○ Robotics Club?

6. ○ Theater or ○ Band?

7. ○ Soccer or ○ Softball?

8. ○ Basketball or ○ Volleyball?

9. ○ Swimming or ○ Track?

10. Write for the ○ Newspaper or ○ Yearbook?

11. When your favorite club holds elections for officer

    positions, are you ○ The first one to raise your hand or

    ○ The one hiding in the back of the room?

12. When you first get home from school, do you

    ○ Grab a snack or ○ Check your e-mail?

13. ○ Do your homework right away ○ Watch TV

    or ○ Hang out with friends first?

14. Who is the first person in the family to get home?

    ○ It's usually me or ○ My parents are already there.

15. ○ Do your chores right away or ○ Put them off

    until the last possible minute?

16. What is your least favorite chore? _____

17. ◯ Walk the dog or ◯ Clean the toilet?

18. ◯ Take out the trash or ◯ Mow the lawn?

19. ◯ Help cook dinner or ◯ Leave it to the adults?

20. ◯ Set the table or ◯ Clear the dishes?

21. When it's time to do the dishes, would you rather

◯ Wash or ◯ Dry?

22. If you take lunch to school, who makes it?

◯ I do or ◯ One of my parents makes it for me.

23. After you've done your homework, would you rather

◯ Talk on the phone or ◯ Chat on the computer?

24. When you're on the computer, do you prefer to

◯ IM with friends or ◯ Surf the Web?

25. My favorite website is _____

26. Would you rather ◯ Read a book or ◯ Flip through

a magazine?

27. My favorite book or magazine is _____

28. Would you rather ◯ Watch TV or ◯ Play video games?

29. What is your favorite TV show? _____

_____

30. What is your favorite video game? _____

_____

Movie Madness
Please silence your cell phones.

1. Would you rather ⬤ Watch a movie in a theater
or ⬤ Curl up on the couch with a DVD?

2. ⬤ Go to the movies with friends or ⬤ Watch a
movie by yourself (no arguments about which one to see!)?

3. Do your parents ⬤ Let you go to the movies by yourself or
⬤ Come with you?

4. Are you allowed to see movies that are rated
PG-13? ⬤ Yes or ⬤ Not yet.

5. ⬤ Romance or ⬤ Action flick?

6. ⬤ Comedy or ⬤ Drama?

7. ⬤ Live action or ⬤ Animated feature?

8. ⬤ IMAX or ⬤ 3-D?

9. Would you rather cry during a movie because it's
⬤ Really sappy and sad or ⬤ Hilariously funny?

10. Snack attack! Do you prefer ⬤ Gummy bears
or ⬤ Swedish Fish?

11. ⬤ Junior Mints or ⬤ Peanut butter cups?

12. ⬤ Snowcaps or ⬤ Licorice?

13. ⬤ Fruity candy or ⬤ Chocolate?

14. Do you like butter on your popcorn? ⬤ Yes, of course! or
⬤ Ick! No way.

15. ⬤ Diet soda or ⬤ Regular?

16. If you could work in the film industry, would you rather be ⬤ An actor or ⬤ A director?

17. A film ⬤ Writer or ⬤ Critic?

18. ⬤ A sound engineer or ⬤ A lighting designer?

19. ⬤ Work on special effects or ⬤ Draw animation?

20. Who is your favorite female actor? _____

21. Who is your favorite male actor? _____

22. What is your favorite movie of all time? _____

23. What is the funniest movie ever? _____

24. The saddest? _____

25. Double features? ⬤ Yes, they're the best! or ⬤ I can't sit still that long!

26. What do you think of previews? ⬤ Love 'em! or ⬤ Hate 'em. I just want to get to the feature!

27. Do you ever forget to turn off your phone in the theater? ⬤ Never! ⬤ Occasionally or ⬤ All the time!

28. Do you text during movies? ⬤ No way! That's totally rude or ⬤ Sure. It's not like I'm making any noise!

29. Is it okay to talk during a movie? ⬤ No. It spoils the movie for others or ⬤ Whispering a little is okay.

30. When the movie ends, do you ⬤ Head straight for the exit or ⬤ Wait until all the credits have rolled?

It's Not Easy Being Green
How environmentally friendly are you?

1. "Being green" refers to ◯ Jealousy or ◯ The environment?

2. ◯ Paper ◯ Plastic or ◯ I bring my own bag?

3. ◯ Bottled water or ◯ Tap water in a reusable bottle?

4. ◯ Shower or ◯ Bath?

5. Is your showerhead ◯ Regular or ◯ Low-flow?

6. When you're brushing your teeth, do you ◯ Let the water run or ◯ Turn it off until you need to rinse?

7. Do you ◯ Hand wash the dishes or ◯ Use the dishwasher?

8. Do you ◯ Use the air conditioner or ◯ Sweat it out?

9. Are your lightbulbs ◯ Regular or ◯ Low-energy?

10. Before you leave, ◯ Turn out the lights or ◯ Leave them on?

11. ◯ Turn off your computer or ◯ Just let it go to sleep?

12. Is your cell phone ◯ Always plugged in or ◯ Only plugged in when it's charging?

13. ◯ Play video games or ◯ Read a book?

14. Are you a ◯ Vegetarian or ◯ Meat eater?

15. If you unwrap a piece of gum while you're outside, do you ◯ Drop the wrapper (it's really small!) or ◯ Put it in your pocket to throw away later?

16. Experiencing nature means ◯ A hike in the woods or

   ◯ A soccer game (hey, it's outdoors!)?

17. Would you rather ◯ Plant a tree or ◯ Sort the recycling?

18. Pick up trash ◯ At a beach or ◯ In a park?

19. Who's greener? ◯ Definitely me ◯ My parents or

   ◯ We're equally concerned about the planet.

20. Which animal are you most worried about: ◯ Whales

   ◯ Polar bears or ◯ Elephants?

21. When it comes to the environment, do you feel

   ◯ Optimistic or ◯ Worried about the future?

22. Do you ◯ Buy a new book or ◯ Borrow one from a friend?

23. How do you get to school? ◯ Take the bus ◯ Walk

   ◯ Ride my bike ◯ My parents drive me or ◯ Carpool

24. Are the plates in your cafeteria ◯ Paper ◯ Plastic or

   ◯ Polystyrene foam?

25. ◯ Brown bag or ◯ Reusable lunchbox?

26. ◯ Cardboard juice box ◯ Thermos or ◯ Reusable bottle?

27. ◯ Fresh fruit and a homemade sandwich or

   ◯ Prepackaged food and snacks?

28. ◯ A handful of potato chips from a big bag or ◯ A small b

29. ◯ I always clear my plate or ◯ There are usually leftovers?

30. Do your food scraps go in the ◯ Compost pile or ◯ Trash c

It's Not Easy Being Green
How environmentally friendly are you?

1. "Being green" refers to ◯ Jealousy or ◯ The environment?

2. ◯ Paper ◯ Plastic or ◯ I bring my own bag?

3. ◯ Bottled water or ◯ Tap water in a reusable bottle?

4. ◯ Shower or ◯ Bath?

5. Is your showerhead ◯ Regular or ◯ Low-flow?

6. When you're brushing your teeth, do you ◯ Let the water run or ◯ Turn it off until you need to rinse?

7. Do you ◯ Hand wash the dishes or ◯ Use the dishwasher?

8. Do you ◯ Use the air conditioner or ◯ Sweat it out?

9. Are your lightbulbs ◯ Regular or ◯ Low-energy?

10. Before you leave, ◯ Turn out the lights or ◯ Leave them on?

11. ◯ Turn off your computer or ◯ Just let it go to sleep?

12. Is your cell phone ◯ Always plugged in or ◯ Only plugged in when it's charging?

13. ◯ Play video games or ◯ Read a book?

14. Are you a ◯ Vegetarian or ◯ Meat eater?

15. If you unwrap a piece of gum while you're outside, do you ◯ Drop the wrapper (it's really small!) or ◯ Put it in your pocket to throw away later?

16. Experiencing nature means ◯ A hike in the woods or
    ◯ A soccer game (hey, it's outdoors!)?

17. Would you rather ◯ Plant a tree or ◯ Sort the recycling?

18. Pick up trash ◯ At a beach or ◯ In a park?

19. Who's greener? ◯ Definitely me ◯ My parents or
    ◯ We're equally concerned about the planet.

20. Which animal are you most worried about: ◯ Whales
    ◯ Polar bears or ◯ Elephants?

21. When it comes to the environment, do you feel
    ◯ Optimistic or ◯ Worried about the future?

22. Do you ◯ Buy a new book or ◯ Borrow one from a friend?

23. How do you get to school? ◯ Take the bus ◯ Walk
    ◯ Ride my bike ◯ My parents drive me or ◯ Carpool

24. Are the plates in your cafeteria ◯ Paper ◯ Plastic or
    ◯ Polystyrene foam?

25. ◯ Brown bag or ◯ Reusable lunchbox?

26. ◯ Cardboard juice box ◯ Thermos or ◯ Reusable bottle?

27. ◯ Fresh fruit and a homemade sandwich or
    ◯ Prepackaged food and snacks?

28. ◯ A handful of potato chips from a big bag or ◯ A small b

29. ◯ I always clear my plate or ◯ There are usually leftovers?

30. Do your food scraps go in the ◯ Compost pile or ◯ Trash c

It's Not Easy Being Green
How environmentally friendly are you?

1. "Being green" refers to ◯ Jealousy or ◯ The environment?

2. ◯ Paper ◯ Plastic or ◯ I bring my own bag?

3. ◯ Bottled water or ◯ Tap water in a reusable bottle?

4. ◯ Shower or ◯ Bath?

5. Is your showerhead ◯ Regular or ◯ Low-flow?

6. When you're brushing your teeth, do you ◯ Let the water run or ◯ Turn it off until you need to rinse?

7. Do you ◯ Hand wash the dishes or ◯ Use the dishwasher?

8. Do you ◯ Use the air conditioner or ◯ Sweat it out?

9. Are your lightbulbs ◯ Regular or ◯ Low-energy?

10. Before you leave, ◯ Turn out the lights or ◯ Leave them on?

11. ◯ Turn off your computer or ◯ Just let it go to sleep?

12. Is your cell phone ◯ Always plugged in or ◯ Only plugged in when it's charging?

13. ◯ Play video games or ◯ Read a book?

14. Are you a ◯ Vegetarian or ◯ Meat eater?

15. If you unwrap a piece of gum while you're outside, do you ◯ Drop the wrapper (it's really small!) or ◯ Put it in your pocket to throw away later?

16. Experiencing nature means ○ A hike in the woods or
    ○ A soccer game (hey, it's outdoors!)?

17. Would you rather ○ Plant a tree or ○ Sort the recycling?

18. Pick up trash ○ At a beach or ○ In a park?

19. Who's greener? ○ Definitely me ○ My parents or
    ○ We're equally concerned about the planet.

20. Which animal are you most worried about: ○ Whales
    ○ Polar bears or ○ Elephants?

21. When it comes to the environment, do you feel
    ○ Optimistic or ○ Worried about the future?

22. Do you ○ Buy a new book or ○ Borrow one from a friend?

23. How do you get to school? ○ Take the bus ○ Walk
    ○ Ride my bike ○ My parents drive me or ○ Carpool

24. Are the plates in your cafeteria ○ Paper ○ Plastic or
    ○ Polystyrene foam?

25. ○ Brown bag or ○ Reusable lunchbox?

26. ○ Cardboard juice box ○ Thermos or ○ Reusable bottle?

27. ○ Fresh fruit and a homemade sandwich or
    ○ Prepackaged food and snacks?

28. ○ A handful of potato chips from a big bag or ○ A small b

29. ○ I always clear my plate or ○ There are usually leftovers?

30. Do your food scraps go in the ○ Compost pile or ○ Trash c

MAKE NEW FRIENDS...
...But keep the old!

1. Making new friends: ○ Easy or ● Hard?

2. Staying close to old friends: ○ Simple or ○ Difficult?

3. Would you introduce a new friend to an old friend?
   ● Absolutely or ○ No way!

4. Why or why not? _Then the old ones have new friend too?_

5. How many new friends have you made in the last year?
   ○ 0-3 ○ 3-6 or ● More than 6

6. Do you call your friends to make plans? ○ Yes, I'm the organizer ○ No or ● It depends.

7. ○ Ice-skate ● Sled or ○ Sip hot chocolate?

8. ● Sing karaoke or ○ Make up funny dance routines?

9. ● Give each other makeovers or ● Play board games?

10. ○ Bake cookies or ○ Play soccer?

11. Would you rather ○ Talk on the phone ● Text or ○ IM?

12. ● See a movie or ○ Go shopping with friends?

13. ○ Have a big group of friends or ● Have a few really close friends?

14. Are your parents your friends? ● Are you kidding? or ○ Totally. They're really cool!

15. Are you friends with your siblings? ● No way! or ● Only when we're not arguing!

16. If a friend is feeling down, would you ⬤ Give her a big hug or ◯ Tell her a funny joke?

17. ⬤ Make a gift or ◯ Buy a gift?

18. Girl's best friend: ⬤ Puppy or ◯ Kitten?

19. There's a new girl in school who seems really cool. Do you ⬤ Invite her to hang out or ◯ Wait for her to approach you?

20. Can boys and girls be friends? ◯ Ew! Gross or ⬤ Sure.

21. ⬤ Be a good listener or ◯ Tell a good story?

22. ⬤ Be kind and trustworthy or ◯ Be cool and popular?

23. ⬤ Always be yourself or ◯ Do what you can to be popular?

24. Do you ever tell someone else's secret? ◯ Never! or ⬤ If it's really juicy.

25. If you fight with your BFF, who says she's sorry? ◯ It's me ◯ She's more forgiving or ⬤ It depends on the situation.

26. ⬤ Invite the new girl to sit with you or ◯ Ignore her?

27. You splash your friend with spaghetti sauce by mistake. Does she ◯ Totally freak out or ⬤ Laugh good-naturedly?

28. Lunch is time to ⬤ Be social or ◯ Catch up on homework?

29. Milk shoots out your friend's nose. Do you ⬤ Laugh along with everyone or ◯ Ask her if she's okay?

30. Your friend forgets her lunch. Do you share yours? ⬤ Definitely or ◯ Only if I'm not that hungry.

MAKE NEW FRIENDS...
...But keep the old!

1. Making new friends: ○ Easy or ○ Hard?

2. Staying close to old friends: ○ Simple or ○ Difficult?

3. Would you introduce a new friend to an old friend?

    ○ Absolutely or ○ No way!

4. Why or why not?_____

5. How many new friends have you made in the last year?

    ○ 0-3 ○ 3-6 or ○ More than 6

6. Do you call your friends to make plans? ○ Yes, I'm the

    organizer ○ No or ○ It depends.

7. ○ Ice-skate ○ Sled or ○ Sip hot chocolate?

8. ○ Sing karaoke or ○ Make up funny dance routines?

9. ○ Give each other makeovers or ○ Play board games?

10. ○ Bake cookies or ○ Play soccer?

11. Would you rather ○ Talk on the phone ○ Text or ○ IM?

12. ○ See a movie or ○ Go shopping with friends?

13. ○ Have a big group of friends or ○ Have a few

    really close friends?

14. Are your parents your friends? ○ Are you kidding? or

    ○ Totally. They're really cool!

15. Are you friends with your siblings? ○ No way! or

    ○ Only when we're not arguing!

16. If a friend is feeling down, would you ○ Give her a big hug or ○ Tell her a funny joke?

17. ○ Make a gift or ○ Buy a gift?

18. Girl's best friend: ○ Puppy or ○ Kitten?

19. There's a new girl in school who seems really cool. Do you ○ Invite her to hang out or ○ Wait for her to approach you?

20. Can boys and girls be friends? ○ Ew! Gross or ○ Sure.

21. ○ Be a good listener or ○ Tell a good story?

22. ○ Be kind and trustworthy or ○ Be cool and popular?

23. ○ Always be yourself or ○ Do what you can to be popular?

24. Do you ever tell someone else's secret? ○ Never! or ○ If it's really juicy.

25. If you fight with your BFF, who says she's sorry? ○ It's me ○ She's more forgiving or ○ It depends on the situation.

26. ○ Invite the new girl to sit with you or ○ Ignore her?

27. You splash your friend with spaghetti sauce by mistake. Does she ○ Totally freak out or ○ Laugh good-naturedly?

28. Lunch is time to ○ Be social or ○ Catch up on homework?

29. Milk shoots out your friend's nose. Do you ○ Laugh along with everyone or ○ Ask her if she's okay?

30. Your friend forgets her lunch. Do you share yours? ○ Definitely or ○ Only if I'm not that hungry.

MAKE NEW FRIENDS...
...But keep the old!

1. Making new friends: ○ Easy or ○ Hard?

2. Staying close to old friends: ○ Simple or ○ Difficult?

3. Would you introduce a new friend to an old friend?

   ○ Absolutely or ○ No way!

4. Why or why not?_____

5. How many new friends have you made in the last year?

   ○ 0-3 ○ 3-6 or ○ More than 6

6. Do you call your friends to make plans? ○ Yes, I'm the

   organizer ○ No or ○ It depends.

7. ○ Ice-skate ○ Sled or ○ Sip hot chocolate?

8. ○ Sing karaoke or ○ Make up funny dance routines?

9. ○ Give each other makeovers or ○ Play board games?

10. ○ Bake cookies or ○ Play soccer?

11. Would you rather ○ Talk on the phone ○ Text or ○ IM?

12. ○ See a movie or ○ Go shopping with friends?

13. ○ Have a big group of friends or ○ Have a few

    really close friends?

14. Are your parents your friends? ○ Are you kidding? or

    ○ Totally. They're really cool!

15. Are you friends with your siblings? ○ No way! or

    ○ Only when we're not arguing!

16. If a friend is feeling down, would you ◯ Give her a big hug or ◯ Tell her a funny joke?

17. ◯ Make a gift or ◯ Buy a gift?

18. Girl's best friend: ◯ Puppy or ◯ Kitten?

19. There's a new girl in school who seems really cool. Do you ◯ Invite her to hang out or ◯ Wait for her to approach you?

20. Can boys and girls be friends? ◯ Ew! Gross or ◯ Sure.

21. ◯ Be a good listener or ◯ Tell a good story?

22. ◯ Be kind and trustworthy or ◯ Be cool and popular?

23. ◯ Always be yourself or ◯ Do what you can to be popular?

24. Do you ever tell someone else's secret? ◯ Never! or ◯ If it's really juicy.

25. If you fight with your BFF, who says she's sorry? ◯ It's me ◯ She's more forgiving or ◯ It depends on the situation.

26. ◯ Invite the new girl to sit with you or ◯ Ignore her?

27. You splash your friend with spaghetti sauce by mistake. Does she ◯ Totally freak out or ◯ Laugh good-naturedly?

28. Lunch is time to ◯ Be social or ◯ Catch up on homework?

29. Milk shoots out your friend's nose. Do you ◯ Laugh along with everyone or ◯ Ask her if she's okay?

30. Your friend forgets her lunch. Do you share yours? ◯ Definitely or ◯ Only if I'm not that hungry.

MaKE NEW FRiENDS...
...But keep the old!

1. Making new friends: ⭕ Easy or ⭕ Hard?

2. Staying close to old friends: ⭕ Simple or ⭕ Difficult?

3. Would you introduce a new friend to an old friend?

   ⭕ Absolutely or ⭕ No way!

4. Why or why not?_____

5. How many new friends have you made in the last year?

   ⭕ 0-3 ⭕ 3-6 or ⭕ More than 6

6. Do you call your friends to make plans? ⭕ Yes, I'm the

   organizer ⭕ No or ⭕ It depends.

7. ⭕ Ice-skate ⭕ Sled or ⭕ Sip hot chocolate?

8. ⭕ Sing karaoke or ⭕ Make up funny dance routines?

9. ⭕ Give each other makeovers or ⭕ Play board games?

10. ⭕ Bake cookies or ⭕ Play soccer?

11. Would you rather ⭕ Talk on the phone ⭕ Text or ⭕ IM?

12. ⭕ See a movie or ⭕ Go shopping with friends?

13. ⭕ Have a big group of friends or ⭕ Have a few

    really close friends?

14. Are your parents your friends? ⭕ Are you kidding? or

    ⭕ Totally. They're really cool!

15. Are you friends with your siblings? ⭕ No way! or

    ⭕ Only when we're not arguing!

16. If a friend is feeling down, would you ○ Give her a big hug or ○ Tell her a funny joke?

17. ○ Make a gift or ○ Buy a gift?

18. Girl's best friend: ○ Puppy or ○ Kitten?

19. There's a new girl in school who seems really cool. Do you ○ Invite her to hang out or ○ Wait for her to approach you?

20. Can boys and girls be friends? ○ Ew! Gross or ○ Sure.

21. ○ Be a good listener or ○ Tell a good story?

22. ○ Be kind and trustworthy or ○ Be cool and popular?

23. ○ Always be yourself or ○ Do what you can to be popular?

24. Do you ever tell someone else's secret? ○ Never! or ○ If it's really juicy.

25. If you fight with your BFF, who says she's sorry? ○ It's me ○ She's more forgiving or ○ It depends on the situation.

26. ○ Invite the new girl to sit with you or ○ Ignore her?

27. You splash your friend with spaghetti sauce by mistake. Does she ○ Totally freak out or ○ Laugh good-naturedly?

28. Lunch is time to ○ Be social or ○ Catch up on homework?

29. Milk shoots out your friend's nose. Do you ○ Laugh along with everyone or ○ Ask her if she's okay?

30. Your friend forgets her lunch. Do you share yours? ○ Definitely or ○ Only if I'm not that hungry.

Dancing Diva

It's time for the school dance!

1. ◯ Ask him to the dance or ◉ Wait for him to ask you?

2. Show up at the dance ◯ By yourself or ◉ With a group of friends?

3. You're on the planning committee. Would you rather ◉ Decorate the gym or ◯ Serve the snacks?

4. Speaking of snacks, what's better: ◉ Popcorn or ◯ Potato chips?

5. ◯ Pizza or ◉ Hot dogs?

6. ◉ Soda or ◯ Punch?

7. ◯ Cookies or ◉ Ice cream?

8. Time for a theme! ◉ '50s sock hop or ◯ Square dance?

9. ◯ Black-and-white gala or ◉ Red carpet Hollywood?

10. Would you rather wear a ◯ Sassy black dress or ◉ Sparkly pink one?

11. ◉ A fun and flirty red dress or ◯ A classic pastel one?

12. ◉ Ballet flats or ◯ Heels?

13. ◯ Jeans and a T-shirt or ◉ A cute top and skirt?

14. Are you allowed to wear makeup to a dance? ◉ Yes ◯ No way! or ◯ Only lip gloss.

15. Will you paint your nails? ◯ Of course! Getting ready is half the fun or ◉ No, I'm more into the natural look.

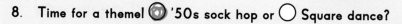

16. What color nail polish? _B w/ Purple sparkles_

17. Hairdo: ● Up or ○ Down?

18. Would you prefer music by a ● DJ or ○ Live band?

19. The next dance is ladies' choice. Do you ask a boy to dance? ● Sure, why not? or ○ No, I'd be too embarrassed!

20. ● Hip-hop or ○ Rock?

21. ○ Pop or ● Techno?

22. ○ "Cotton-Eyed Joe" or ● "Macarena"?

23. ● "The Cha Cha Slide" or ○ "Electric Slide"?

24. ○ Slow dance or ● Fast?

25. What's your favorite song? _Stronger_

26. Who's your favorite singer? _Kelly Clarson_

27. What's your favorite band? _____

28. ● Girl groups or ○ Boy bands?

29. When a slow song comes on, do you ● Head for the snack table or ○ Ask your crush to dance?

30. Who would you most like to dance with? _____

Dancing Diva

It's time for the school dance!

1. ○ Ask him to the dance or ○ Wait for him to ask you?

2. Show up at the dance ○ By yourself or ○ With a group of friends?

3. You're on the planning committee. Would you rather ○ Decorate the gym or ○ Serve the snacks?

4. Speaking of snacks, what's better: ○ Popcorn or ○ Potato chips?

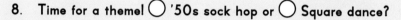

5. ○ Pizza or ○ Hot dogs?

6. ○ Soda or ○ Punch?

7. ○ Cookies or ○ Ice cream?

8. Time for a theme! ○ '50s sock hop or ○ Square dance?

9. ○ Black-and-white gala or ○ Red carpet Hollywood?

10. Would you rather wear a ○ Sassy black dress or ○ Sparkly pink one?

11. ○ A fun and flirty red dress or ○ A classic pastel one?

12. ○ Ballet flats or ○ Heels?

13. ○ Jeans and a T-shirt or ○ A cute top and skirt?

14. Are you allowed to wear makeup to a dance? ○ Yes ○ No way! or ○ Only lip gloss.

15. Will you paint your nails? ○ Of course! Getting ready is half the fun or ○ No, I'm more into the natural look.

16. What color nail polish?_____

17. Hairdo: ⃝ Up or ⃝ Down?

18. Would you prefer music by a ⃝ DJ or ⃝ Live band?

19. The next dance is ladies' choice. Do you ask a boy to
    dance? ⃝ Sure, why not? or ⃝ No, I'd be too embarrassed!

20. ⃝ Hip-hop or ⃝ Rock?

21. ⃝ Pop or ⃝ Techno?

22. ⃝ "Cotton-Eyed Joe" or ⃝ "Macarena"?

23. ⃝ "The Cha Cha Slide" or ⃝ "Electric Slide"?

24. ⃝ Slow dance or ⃝ Fast?

25. What's your favorite song? _____

26. Who's your favorite singer? _____

27. What's your favorite band? _____

28. ⃝ Girl groups or ⃝ Boy bands?

29. When a slow song comes on, do you ⃝ Head for the
    snack table or ⃝ Ask your crush to dance?

30. Who would you most like to dance with? _____

Dancing Diva

It's time for the school dance!

1. ○ Ask him to the dance or ○ Wait for him to ask you?

2. Show up at the dance ○ By yourself or ○ With a group of friends?

3. You're on the planning committee. Would you rather ○ Decorate the gym or ○ Serve the snacks?

4. Speaking of snacks, what's better: ○ Popcorn or ○ Potato chips?

5. ○ Pizza or ○ Hot dogs?

6. ○ Soda or ○ Punch?

7. ○ Cookies or ○ Ice cream?

8. Time for a theme! ○ '50s sock hop or ○ Square dance?

9. ○ Black-and-white gala or ○ Red carpet Hollywood?

10. Would you rather wear a ○ Sassy black dress or ○ Sparkly pink one?

11. ○ A fun and flirty red dress or ○ A classic pastel one?

12. ○ Ballet flats or ○ Heels?

13. ○ Jeans and a T-shirt or ○ A cute top and skirt?

14. Are you allowed to wear makeup to a dance? ○ Yes ○ No way! or ○ Only lip gloss.

15. Will you paint your nails? ○ Of course! Getting ready is half the fun or ○ No, I'm more into the natural look.

16. What color nail polish? _____

17. Hairdo: ◯ Up or ◯ Down?

18. Would you prefer music by a ◯ DJ or ◯ Live band?

19. The next dance is ladies' choice. Do you ask a boy to
    dance? ◯ Sure, why not? or ◯ No, I'd be too embarrassed!

20. ◯ Hip-hop or ◯ Rock?

21. ◯ Pop or ◯ Techno?

22. ◯ "Cotton-Eyed Joe" or ◯ "Macarena"?

23. ◯ "The Cha Cha Slide" or ◯ "Electric Slide"?

24. ◯ Slow dance or ◯ Fast?

25. What's your favorite song? _____

26. Who's your favorite singer? _____

27. What's your favorite band? _____

28. ◯ Girl groups or ◯ Boy bands?

29. When a slow song comes on, do you ◯ Head for the
    snack table or ◯ Ask your crush to dance?

30. Who would you most like to dance with? _____

Dancing Diva

It's time for the school dance!

1. ○ Ask him to the dance or ○ Wait for him to ask you?
2. Show up at the dance ○ By yourself or ○ With a group of friends?
3. You're on the planning committee. Would you rather ○ Decorate the gym or ○ Serve the snacks?
4. Speaking of snacks, what's better: ○ Popcorn or ○ Potato chips?
5. ○ Pizza or ○ Hot dogs?
6. ○ Soda or ○ Punch?
7. ○ Cookies or ○ Ice cream?
8. Time for a theme! ○ '50s sock hop or ○ Square dance?
9. ○ Black-and-white gala or ○ Red carpet Hollywood?
10. Would you rather wear a ○ Sassy black dress or ○ Sparkly pink one?
11. ○ A fun and flirty red dress or ○ A classic pastel one?
12. ○ Ballet flats or ○ Heels?
13. ○ Jeans and a T-shirt or ○ A cute top and skirt?
14. Are you allowed to wear makeup to a dance? ○ Yes ○ No way! or ○ Only lip gloss.
15. Will you paint your nails? ○ Of course! Getting ready is half the fun or ○ No, I'm more into the natural look.

16. What color nail polish?_____

17. Hairdo: ◯ Up or ◯ Down?

18. Would you prefer music by a ◯ DJ or ◯ Live band?

19. The next dance is ladies' choice. Do you ask a boy to dance? ◯ Sure, why not? or ◯ No, I'd be too embarrassed!

20. ◯ Hip-hop or ◯ Rock?

21. ◯ Pop or ◯ Techno?

22. ◯ "Cotton-Eyed Joe" or ◯ "Macarena"?

23. ◯ "The Cha Cha Slide" or ◯ "Electric Slide"?

24. ◯ Slow dance or ◯ Fast?

25. What's your favorite song? _____

26. Who's your favorite singer? _____

27. What's your favorite band? _____

28. ◯ Girl groups or ◯ Boy bands?

29. When a slow song comes on, do you ◯ Head for the snack table or ◯ Ask your crush to dance?

30. Who would you most like to dance with? _____

TRUE BLUE

How well do you know your BFF?
Answer these questions the way you think your BFF
would reply. Then swap and see how you both did!

. How long have you been friends? _Almos forcver_

. How did you meet? _Backyards_

. ◯ Always on time ◯ Usually late or ⦿ 50/50?

. What is she most afraid of? _spiders_

. Does she sleep with a stuffed animal? ◯ R U serious?

⦿ Yes, totally.

. What is her best quality? _Being nice_

. Is she ⦿ Outgoing and talkative or ◯ Shy and quiet?

. What's her favorite color? _Blue/green_

. What would she say is worse: ⦿ Getting in a fight

with you or ◯ Getting a bad grade?

. ⦿ Not being able to watch TV for a week or ⦿ Not

being able to talk on the phone?

. Would she rather ⦿ Go to the beach or ◯ Spend time

exploring a big city?

. ◯ Go for a hike in the woods or ⦿ Visit a museum?

. ⦿ Be a scientist or ◯ Write novels one day?

. ⦿ Play a sport or ⦿ Take an art class?

. ◯ Go to the movie theater with a big group of kids or

⦿ Stay in and watch a movie with just one friend?

16. What's her favorite ice cream flavor? _chocolet_

17. Is she a ⊘ Meat eater or a ◯ Vegetarian?

18. What's her favorite pizza topping? _peperoni_

19. Is she the kind of person who sings in the shower?

    ⊘ Probably ◯ I doubt it or ◯ I have no idea.

20. If she's just had a terrible day, is she more likely to

    ◯ Keep it to herself or ⊘ Call to talk to you about it?

21. Does she prefer ◯ Girly skirts ⊘ No-nonsense jeans or

    ◯ A mix of both?

22. What's her favorite electronic gadget: ◯ Her iPod or

    ⊘ Her cell phone?

23. Her locker is ◯ A pigsty or ⊘ Neater and more organized

    than the school library?

24. Does she cry easily? ◯ Yes, she's sensitive or

    ⊘ Nope, she's really tough.

25. Does she prefer ⊘ Staying up late or ◯ Rising early?

26. Would she ⊘ Read the book or ◯ Watch the movie?

27. What's her favorite book? _____

28. What's her favorite movie? _____

29. Does she have a crush? ⊘ Eeeeek! Yes! or

    ⊘ I don't think so?

30. If so, what's her crush's name? _____

TRUE BLUE

How well do you know your BFF?
Answer these questions the way you think your BFF would reply. Then swap and see how you both did!

1. How long have you been friends? _____

2. How did you meet? _____

3. ◯ Always on time ◯ Usually late or ◯ 50/50?

4. What is she most afraid of? _____

5. Does she sleep with a stuffed animal? ◯ R U serious?
   ◯ Yes, totally.

6. What is her best quality? _____

7. Is she ◯ Outgoing and talkative or ◯ Shy and quiet?

8. What's her favorite color? _____

9. What would she say is worse: ◯ Getting in a fight
   with you or ◯ Getting a bad grade?

10. ◯ Not being able to watch TV for a week or ◯ Not
    being able to talk on the phone?

11. Would she rather ◯ Go to the beach or ◯ Spend time
    exploring a big city?

12. ◯ Go for a hike in the woods or ◯ Visit a museum?

13. ◯ Be a scientist or ◯ Write novels one day?

14. ◯ Play a sport or ◯ Take an art class?

15. ◯ Go to the movie theater with a big group of kids or
    ◯ Stay in and watch a movie with just one friend?

16. What's her favorite ice cream flavor? _____

17. Is she a ⭕ Meat eater or a ⭕ Vegetarian?

18. What's her favorite pizza topping? _____

19. Is she the kind of person who sings in the shower?

    ⭕ Probably ⭕ I doubt it or ⭕ I have no idea.

20. If she's just had a terrible day, is she more likely to

    ⭕ Keep it to herself or ⭕ Call to talk to you about it?

21. Does she prefer ⭕ Girly skirts ⭕ No-nonsense jeans or

    ⭕ A mix of both?

22. What's her favorite electronic gadget: ⭕ Her iPod or

    ⭕ Her cell phone?

23. Her locker is ⭕ A pigsty or ⭕ Neater and more organized

    than the school library?

24. Does she cry easily? ⭕ Yes, she's sensitive or

    ⭕ Nope, she's really tough.

25. Does she prefer ⭕ Staying up late or ⭕ Rising early?

26. Would she ⭕ Read the book or ⭕ Watch the movie?

27. What's her favorite book? _____

28. What's her favorite movie? _____

29. Does she have a crush? ⭕ Eeeeek! Yes! or

    ⭕ I don't think so?

30. If so, what's her crush's name? _____